The 51st State: A Libertarian path for Puerto Rico's Economic Revival and Statehood

Politics, Volume 1

Jose Rivera Neris

Published by Jose Rivera Neris, 2025.

THE 51ST STATE: A LIBERTARIAN PATH FOR PUERTO RICO'S ECONOMIC REVIVAL AND STATEHOOD

First edition. July 25, 2025.

ISBN: 979-8231009565

Written by Jose Rivera Neris.

Also by Jose Rivera Neris

Politics
The 51st State: A Libertarian path for Puerto Rico's Economic Revival and Statehood

Social Studies
The Facts, Ethics, and Culture of Strip Clubs

Table of Contents

"The 51st State: | A Libertarian path for Puerto Rico's Economic Revival and Statehood" 1

Foundations of Liberty, Economy, and Governance 3

Core Economic Concepts 7

Introduction: | The Intersection of Freedom and Statehood 11

Part I: Diagnosing the Crisis 15

Chapter 1: The Cost of Dependency 19

Chapter 2: Energy Woes and Infrastructure Decay 23

Part II: Embracing Economic Freedom 27

Chapter 3: Tax Reform and Entrepreneurial Incentives 31

Chapter 4: Privatization and Deregulation 35

Part III: The Case for Statehood 41

Chapter 5: Addressing Concerns and Misconceptions 47

Cultural Self-Determination in Statehood: | The New Mexico Example for Puerto Rico 53

Conclusion: | A Guide To Freedom And Wealth 57

Chapter 6: Civic Renewal and Institutional Reform 59

Chapter 7: Education, Human Capital, and Self-Reliance 63

Chapter 8: Building the 51st State: A Strategic Roadmap 67

Chapter 9: | Support for Statehood - Puerto Ricos Referendums 71

Chapter 10: Libertarian Political Platform for Puerto Rico 75

Chapter 11: Where Libertarianism Has Worked 81

The Honorable Officials of Puerto Rico and Their Colleagues in the United States Congress | A Call for Bold Action on Puerto Ricos Future For Liberty, Prosperity, and Mutual Benefit 87

Guest Collaboration | Political Status and Economic Liberty: | A Libertarian View on Puerto Rico's Labyrinth 91

Dedication

This is for the people of Puerto Rico, who have waited far too long to be seen and heard.

For the supporters of statehood who still push through years of silence, fake politics, and broken promises, refusing to settle until Puerto Rico stands beside the fifty states not as a colony, but as a respectful partner in the United States family.

For anyone who turns their back on the idea of second-class citizenship becoming permanent and who pictures a tomorrow when every Puerto Rican shares the same rights, chores, and shield of law that other Americans take for granted.

For all the libertarians, individualists, and watchful defenders of personal freedom, the people who see that real justice comes not from bigger government but from honoring each person's right to choose, work, speak, dream, and rise as high as hard effort allows.

And to everyone who knows that fairness isn't a prize dropped in our laps but something people make happen by insisting on better, this work is for you. I hope it becomes more than just talk, I hope it nudges you to get involved.

Very Respectfully

Jose Rivera Neris

"The 51st State:
A Libertarian path for Puerto Rico's Economic Revival and Statehood"

Jose Rivera Neris

"We want and we ask for equality,"-
José Celso Barbosa

Foundations of Liberty, Economy, and Governance

Foundations of Liberty, Economy, and Governance

A fresh start for Puerto Rico begins with the words we choose. Long before budgets or ballots catch our eye, we ought to pause at freedom, economy, and government. Is liberty the same thing as raw license? Is capitalism simply a polite name for cronyism? People may call it hair-splitting, yet the little things usually bite first.

The chapter sketches a rough foundation. Libertarianism, for instance, boils down to the idea that free people and small-handed rulers belong at the center of every public payroll. Next, we note federalism, the rule of law, and those democratic brakes meant to keep extremism honest. Finally, we run through the big-name economists-classical, Keynesian, Austrian, Chicago, and even Marx-because each set of goggles sees different roads to prosperity and justice.

Libertarianism: Freedom at the Core

Libertarian thought starts with the old notion that personal freedom beats almost every other goal a government might brag about. The view insists that state power exists chiefly to guard our rights, not to nudge, dictate, or cradle us. That means keeping taxes and red tape light enough for regular folks to walk without tripping.

A free-market ethos strolls right alongside the slimmed-down state. In this picture, deals made between grown-ups' fuel innovation and, yes, the occasional stumble, too. A dependable rule of law stitches the whole thing together, making sure the same rules apply to the banker, the teacher, and the politician-though history tells us the last group sometimes needs the lesson drilled twice.

Some thinkers keep popping up in libertarian reading lists. John Locke catalogued life, liberty, and property, then insisted government had to honor all three. Friedrich Hayek warned that too much central planning smothers the messier-but-healthy pattern he called spontaneous order. Milton Friedman argued the safety net shouldn't balloon past what markets cant cover. Finally,

Robert Nozick condensed his views into a slim book that many think put modern libertarianism on the map. Collectivist ideologies-socialist, progressive, authoritarian alike-pull the state to the center and push the individual off to the side. Libertarians draw the opposite line.

SOVEREIGNTY VS. SUBSIDIARITY

Every talk about political borders circles back to the idea that a realm gets to govern itself. But followers of subsidiarity say the closest level of authority is usually the wisest one. Distant apparatchiks lose credibility faster than they gain it.

FEDERALISM

A federal structure carves up responsibility between a national seat and regional corners. Puerto Rico, for instance, can settle its own affairs while still tapping the federal safety net. That split keeps power from nesting comfortably in one place.

RULE OF LAW

Liberty survives when laws bind officials instead of citizens. Courts must stand apart from the whims of the loudest voice in the room, statutes must be applied fairly no matter who walks in the door, and politicians must know they cannot use law as a switchblade.

DEMOCRACY AND CONSTITUTIONALISM

Voting lets a majority signal its preferences, yet an unchecked majority can trample the lonely few. A strong constitution-well, the framers thought it should be microscopic for minorities and broad on due process-works to steady the scale.

Core Economic Concepts

1. Capitalism and Free Markets

At its heart, capitalism rests on private ownership and the plain urge to turn a profit. Mix in free markets, where people buy and sell with little red tape, and you've got a restless engine that keeps spitting out new ideas.

2. Central Planning

Central planning flips that picture; the government, not a crowd of shoppers, decides who makes what and at what price. Critics from the Libertarian camp warn that such control smothers the sparks that drive growth.

3. Economic Freedom

Economic freedom is the simple right to earn, spend, hire, launch a startup, or stash cash away for a rainy day. Think tanks like the Fraser Institute try to pin that slippery concept down in an annual scorecard called the Economic Freedom of the World Index.

4. Cronyism and Regulatory Capture

Trouble shows up when insiders rig the rules-with agencies and corporations teaming up to kneecap rivals or to milk taxpayers for easy money. In those moments, the level playing field dissolves, and fair competition becomes a quaint slogan.

Schools of Economic Thought: A Brief Survey

A. Classical Economics

Classical thinkers such as Adam Smith pictured an invisible hands-steering markets toward balance while people acted in their own interest. Their faith in specialization, free trade, and modest government remains a set of guiding principles for many economists today.[1]

B. Keynesian Economics

John Maynard Keynes saw the broader economy slipping into stagnation when confidence wobbled, so he called for deliberate government spending and agile monetary moves to jolt demand back to life. That big-picture approach still shapes cash-policy meetings and budget debates alike.[2]

C. Austrian Economics

Carl Menger, Ludwig von Mises, and Friedrich Hayek laid the groundwork. Their followers celebrate the messiness of human choice, rely on price signals, and eye central planners with deep suspicion. For them, living, breathing action drives the economy, not a spreadsheet. [3]

D. Chicago School

Milton Friedman casts a long shadow here. His monetarist prescriptions and call for sweeping deregulation insist that economic freedom and political freedom are twins. In his view, when government oversteps, the dollar-and-cents order tips out of balance.[4]

E. Marxist Economics

Karl Marx saw capitalism as built on quiet exploitation and predicted that class struggle would shove workers into seizing ownership for the common good. Detractors abound, yet wrestling with his critique sharpens any economics lens. [5]

Why These Ideas Matter for Puerto Rico

Words like freedom or sovereignty have hefted in the real world. If freedom means a drab central plan, poverty crowds in. If sovereignty morphs into federal micromanagement, local voices are swallowed whole. If economic liberty lives beneath a mountain of red tape, fresh opportunity sits still. Modern schools of thought offer clues to the archipelago's education failures, its state-run energy fumbles, and the sluggish export lanes. Washington arguments on statehood, tax breaks, or competition policy hinge on how we frame governance and markets. Steering Puerto Rico toward robust prosperity will mean picking one of these intellectual road maps instead of skirting the debate.

A Compass, Not a Map

Think of these pages as a compass, not a turn-by-turn guide. Weve lined up ideas on Puerto Rican stagnation, road-worn infrastructure, and the stirrings of local political spirit. Each definition you circle back to will steady the hand as bolder plans-such as spinning off PREPA, widening school options, or sketching a freer post-statehood constitution-move from chalkboard to public debate.

None of that will click if clarity slips away. Real talk about freedom, a working economy, and genuine sovereignty has to stay at the center while the reforms start rolling out. Otherwise, the fresh road might lead straight back to the old dead end.

Introduction:
The Intersection of Freedom and Statehood

Introduction:

The Intersection of Freedom and Statehood

Puerto Rico is at a critical crossroads in its history, sandwiched between a history of colonial rule and the desire to fully integrate as a state within the United States. Looking ahead to 2025, the island grapples with a unique blend of economic growth alongside enduring structural hurdles. While progress is being made with recovery from prior financial crises marked by the stabilization of household debt and increasing private sector employment, persistent challenges such as soaring energy costs, emigration, and public sector inefficiencies remain constrictive to growth. These economic challenges cannot be separated from Puerto Rico's unresolved political status, which provides limited access to active participation in American democracy while subjecting Puerto Rico to federal mandates without fair representation. [6]

This book defends the position that the statehood of Puerto Rico is not only an issue of civil rights and democratic participation but also a significant milestone toward constructing a freer, more responsible, and prosperous society. Looking from a libertarian approach, the current territorial status is a disadvantage to individual freedom, market access, and self-rule since it places Puerto Rico under an ambiguous structure of federal supervision. Statehood affords the unambiguous framework and constitutional guarantees needed to achieve balanced budgets, secure property rights, and eliminate the bureaucratic dependence that has eroded economic dynamism. [7] Yet statehood, by itself, is not enough. It has to be intertwined with systemic changes based on the free market, minimal state interference, and civic responsibility. As Cato Institute and Students for Liberty scholars have pointed out, Puerto Rico also needs to strengthen its constitutional frameworks, adopt balanced budget amendments, and concentrate fiscal powers to make room for innovation and entrepreneurship. [8] This book aims to diagram Puerto Rico's metamorphosis around three pivotal axes. Part I discusses the island's economy and public finances, outlining its challenges and the potential opportunities unlocked by statehood.

Part II foregrounds representation, constitutional rights, governance reform, and the other political and legal ramifications of statehood. III put forth a libertarian Puerto Rican policy, which included maquiladora program openings, regulatory relaxations on local businesses, additional school choice programs for Puerto Rican students, and a deregulated energy market. The remainder of the book integrates data from Puerto Ricans, economists, and policymakers, alongside government and expert reports.

This vision presents Puerto Rico as a thriving state rather than a dependent region by combining libertarian ideologies with the economic reality. I see the residents empowered by responsibility and freedom, claiming dominion over their future shaped by self-reliance and self-determination. This vision deeply aligns with Puerto Rico's historical arc and its unfolding narrative.

Part I: Diagnosing the Crisis

The Colonial History of Puerto Rico and Its Economic Conditions

The present economic difficulties of Puerto Rico can be traced back to its colonial history and political status. Puerto Rico has been a US territory since 1898, and the island has had a complicated relationship with the continent, merging superficially integrated governance with economic appropriation. In this chapter, we look at Puerto Rico's history during the time of colonization, the effects of imperialistic policies on its economy, and the fallout of restricted suffrage.

Puerto Rico's Territorial Status: A Brief Historical Overview

Puerto Rico became an official US territory after the Treaty of Paris on 1898 following the Spanish American War. Initially under military governance, the island's political system changed with the Foraker Act of 1900 which created a civilian government while still retaining considerable authority with the US Congress. The Jones-Shafroth Act of 1917 provided Puerto Ricans with US citizenship, however, without full political rights including representation in Congress and the ability to cast votes in presidential elections. This seized unincorporated territorial status has continued to exist.

Colonization and Puerto Rico's Economic Development

The colonial relationship with the United States has particularly impacted the economy of the Puerto Rico. In the early 20th century, policies from the United States promoted the establishment of large sugar plantations resulting in the local farmer's displacement and wealth concentration. [9] The economy of the island became dependent on a handful of export industries which dominated the economy, increasing the vulnerability to economic recessions. [10] In the mid-20th century, Operation Bootstrap sought to industrialize Puerto Rico through the establishment of American companies by offering tax breaks and cheap labor.

Although some economic growth occurred, there was an overreliance on foreign investment, and the economy did not evolve into a diversified, self-sustaining economy. The removal of tax benefits towards the end of the 1990s contributed to a reduction in manufacturing and a rise in unemployment. [11] In addition, the island's inability to use Chapter 9 bankruptcy protections like US states deepened Puerto Rico's debt crisis. The creation of the Financial Oversight and Management Board (FOMB) through the PROMESA Act in 2016 gave Puerto Rico no local control over its budget since the board, composed of external, unpaid officials, was granted sweeping control of the island's finances. [12]

Consequences of Limited Political Representation

The lack of voting representation in Congress coupled with absence from presidential elections carries dire consequences on governance and socio-economic prosperity. In the absence of full representation, the island possesses no meaningful leverage over federal policies which directly impact the economy and infrastructure. Such disenfranchisement fuels the politics of identity and marginalization for Puerto Ricans. [13]

Without proper representation, the federal response to natural disasters has also been impacted. Taking Hurricane Maria of 2017 as an example, the disaster was largely viewed as neglected in comparison to aid provided to the mainland. The sluggish response highlighted the consequences stemming from Puerto Rico's territorial status. The island's lack of political status complicates the treatment of federal programs, bringing unequal funding to health care, education, and infrastructure. This imbalance impairs the island's efforts in tackling and resolving its socio-economic issues.

Conclusion

The stagnant economy of Puerto Rico cannot be fully grasped if not analyzed with the colonial history and contemporary political situation in mind. The restricted self-governance and absence of complete political representation has hindered Puerto Rico's economic development and resilient response to crises. Solving such structural challenges is fundamental in Puerto Rico's development towards achieving sustainable growth that guarantees fair treatment for Puerto Ricans. Strengthening the systemic solutions to the challenges Puerto Rico faces anchored in colonial history demands rethinking its political ties with the United States, considering even statehood.

Chapter 1: The Cost of Dependency

The political status of Puerto Rico has shaped its economy along with its dependency on federal funding, trade restrictions, and other strict regulations. All of these have limited the island's economic freedom and potential for growth.

Federal Assistance and Its Impact on Local Governance

Puerto Rico has been receiving federal assistance which has been beneficial, albeit simultaneously burdensome. Support is often accompanied by suffocating federal conditions which stifle local self-governance. Puerto Rico suffered from Hurricane Maria in 2017, and Congress pledged 62 billion for relief funding. While the funding was earmarked, Puerto Rico faced significant (FOMB) micromanaging the entire process to unparalleled extremes. [14] As of September 2021, only 62 billion for relief funding. Puerto Rico faced significant delays in receiving access to it due to the Financial Oversight and Management Board (FOMB) micromanaging the entire process to unparalleled extremes.1 As of September 2021, only 18 billion had been released. Additionally, Puerto Rico has grown ever increasingly reliant on federal aid. Between 2010 and 2020, federal aid increased from 26 to 42 percent of Puerto Rico's GNP. During this timeline, Puerto Rico went from receiving 26% of gross national product through federal aid to receiving 42%, reinforcing the perception of over-dependence eroding structural autonomy.[15]

Restricting Trade and Shipping Under the Jones Act

Known as the Jones Act, the Merchant Marine Act of 1920 restricted transportation between US ports with vessels only if the vessels were American owned, built, or crewed. Puerto Rico suffers from this act as shipping costs have skyrocketed alongside the unnecessary price tag for goods and services derived from its association with America. Estimates from the Cato Institute suggest the Jones Act Cruises charges Puerto Rican shipping companies an additional $568.9 million every year, which consumes 1.1 Billion dollars of consumer money every year in total. [16]

These increased expenses have a lot of spending effects as well. Puerto Rico imports almost 85% food, so the importing portion of the food is definitely going to increase the living standards. Plus, now and then, during emergencies the Jones act has the ability to delay the delivery of some critical supplies like it took place post hurricane Fiona 2022. For example, foreign vessels had to be legally allowed to deliver lot of natural gas (LNG) to Puerto Rican shores.[17]

How America's Federal Regulations Contribute to The Lag in Economic Growth

Apart from the trade barriers put in place, there are also Puerto Rico-specific regulations that have limited the Economic Growth of the region. For the islands, there is a strange mix of America laws that treats them differently. For example, Puerto Rico does not get minimum wage exempted which increases business infrastructure, however, it instead makes purchasing power lower for them. Then, the federal taxes put on income, capital and business construction is way higher than compared to America ratios, so even while trying to stimulate the economy, the island's taxes will bring the opposite effects.[18]

On top of that, there are too many of such laws regarding special licensing for certain professions which further complicate the business environment. Research conducted by the University of Puerto Rico indicates that more than 140 occupations are regulated on the island and at least 131 have some form of active regulation. Of particular note is that 34 of these licenses are required in less than five US states and 13 of them are unique to Puerto Rico. Such stringent licensing can hinder employment opportunities and entrepreneurial activities leading to a decrease in economic dynamism.

Conclusion

Puerto Rico's political status and related dependencies on federal funding, trade restrictions like the Jones Act, and intricate regulatory frameworks intertwine with the island's economic woes. These elements have, in unison, constrained the island's economic independence and autonomy. Resolving these challenges calls for a complete rethink of Puerto Rico's governing policies and the need to reduce austerity while increasing self-determination, thereby fostering sustainable growth.

Chapter 2: Energy Woes and Infrastructure Decay

The energy crisis affecting Puerto Rico and the decay of its infrastructure represent the most degraded challenges on the island's long-term sustainable self-sufficiency and economic growth. These problems arise from a deep-seated neglect throughout the years combined with Puerto Rico's peculiar colonial status, diminished self-governance, and reliance on federally unregulated monopolistic systems. The energy framework operates within a territory that is dominated federally and so is severely outdated, inefficient, and expensive, causing diminished social cohesion opportunities within Puerto Rico. This scenario also provides the best opportunities for advanced technological innovations to be developed within Puerto Rico's SMEAT region, especially the use of modular nuclear reactors (SMRs) and the expansion of photovoltaic solar power use.

The Energy Crisis: Symptoms of a Deeper Problem

The Puerto Rican energy sector has traditionally exhibited centralization, an reliance on imported fuel, and the Puerto Rico Electric Power Authority (PREPA)- a government monopoly's operational ineptitude. Puerto Rico is highly susceptible to price shocks and supply chain disruptions as around 97% of his electricity is imported in the form of fossil fuels. Power outages, old infrastructure, poor management, and-power- and misadministration ultimately led to the grid system failure after Maria in 2017, which left some regions incapacitated for electricity access for close to a year. The consequences in consideration are quite deep. Household strain measure against stifled small business development which further escalates reduced competitiveness owing to high expenses on energy. Puerto Rico's residential electricity prices in 2022 were among the highest in the United States, measuring up to almost 20 cents per kilowatt-hour while the national average rested at around 13 cents. This has deepened the energy security constraints and worsened the gap that exists economically and socially. [19]:

The contract with LUMA Energy to manage PREPA's transmission and distribution system has been advertised as part of reform initiatives, but it remains contentious. LUMA is widely criticized for service interruptions added to not fully meeting reliability or cost-efficiency targets and lack of transparency. Furthermore, they were not able to significantly improve reliability or cost-efficiency. [20] It is difficult to claim that the problem lies in who operates the grid. It is the system's market structure that is the issue. A controlled, bureaucratically monopolized system—public or private will continue to fail without a competition to fight against and decentralization.

Infrastructure Collapse and Its Ripple Effects

The energy concern about Puerto Rico is linked to an infrastructure problem that the island is facing. Years of maintaining infrastructure have been neglected because of bureaucracy, inefficiency, and ineffective spending. Puerto Rico's roads, transport, public water systems, and bridges are obsolete. After Maria, FEMA (Federal Emergency Management Agency) post-willingly provided billions in recovery funding, but progress has been extremely slow because of corruption, red tapes, and administrative overlap at the local level. Puerto Rico's deterioration of infrastructural facilities includes energy, transport, and water services which pose a significant problem for both indigenous businesses and international firms. Schools and hospitals, as well as essential emergency services, remain a risk. Puerto Rico lacks the self-sustaining economic potential. Apart from being digitally and physically connected, the state requires a strategically competitive economy.

Toward a Freer Market: Innovation and Decentralization

Puerto Rico's governance system is not efficient. It should undergo a complete overhaul and implement a systematic change in the setup and management of energy infrastructure. Such changes include establishing an open-access market and loosening government control over the distribution and generation of energy. Giving more providers, from large scale renewable companies to local energy cooperatives, access to power will break PREPA's monopolistic control, allowing for more competition. On the other hand, the moderation system must provide funding for new technologies like microgrids, battery storage, or modern nuclear options such as Small Modular Reactors (SMRs), which can be relied on for constant scalable emissions-free energy. The potential of nuclear energy can be seen through the eyes of Puerto Rico's energy future as a controversial but powerful option. Unlike traditional nuclear facilities, modern SMRs are safer and more cost-efficient. Additionally, they don't take up as much land. Their adoption would greatly assist with powering the industrial sector and solar and wind powered renewables would allow it to function as a stabilizer for the energy grid.

Sola's position within the island, together with the presence of wind boosts Puerto Rico's energy opportunity, with the use of cost-efficient solar facilities such as towers. The presence of Elon Musk's Powerwall battery systems already give Tangible evidence for greater utilization of energy discharge devices. Unfortunately, policies incentivize people to evade taking part in further self-sustainment powered with fossil fuels. Puerto Rico bypassing tax incentives, simplifies policies linked to grid connection, this will permit the Territory to further stand out worldwide with the sharp reduction in energy dependency that stems from geo-politics.

Market Growth Accompanied by Statehood and Sovereignty

The energy crisis is a symptom of a more serious problem that stems from colonial-style government and markets. While there is some value in the federal government providing aid, long-term recovery and prosperity depends on federal policies that provide structural change. Any future policy direction must have at its core focus the reform of energy markets and the adoption of new technologies. Statehood would provide Puerto Rico the certainty they need to implement these changes and additionally guarantee the full access of Puerto Rican constituents to federal energy facility programs. In the end, what is required is a more laissez-faire market approach to do away with an economically suppressed Puerto Rico, one that is vibrant, innovative, and energy secure.

Part II: Embracing Economic Freedom

The Libertarian Vision for Prosperity

Puerto Rico's overreliance on federal aid, which has hurt its economy and led to rampant misuse of funds, Puerto Rico sits at a crossroad. The first option is a constantly placed oversight and aid marked by attention grabbing policies and central planning. The second option, which creates liberty is characterized by economic freedom, personal responsibility, localization, and empowerment. Los Pueblos needs to shed its dependency model to embrace a libertarian vision. This self-sustaining ideology guides Puerto Rico towards prosperity.

Free Markets, Individual Liberty, and Limited Government

The essence of libertarian thought is when the caretaking of an individual is taken over by a bureaucracy service. That is accompanied by economic and political institutions that stem from it. In simple terms, institutional economics - citizens have the greatest ability to make life decisions regarding their lives, along with their earnings and trades. Economic freedom includes a wide variety of voluntary exchange, protected property rights, regulations imposed, controlled taxes, and an overall less active government intervention in economics. These principles stimulate new ideas, draw funding, and establish an infrastructure favorable for business endeavors. Subsequently, stifled markets sprinkled with government control or red tape can nurture rise in standard of living which is often overlooked by aided schemes.

For a long time, Milton Friedman and Friedrich Hayek have argued in favor of unregulated markets, claiming that free markets create, both in terms of morality and function, more efficiency than government designed systems.[21] We could use all these unregulated frills to describe Puerto Rico, which has wasted public funds, received unneeded subsidies, maintained meticulous amounts of bureaucracy, and witnessed the decline of enterprise as the government took the center stage. Instead, local vigor can be released through prudent policies aimed at inspiring economic growth, instead of suffocating it with dependency and unnecessary regulations.

Global Examples of Liberalization and Growth

The advantages of liberalization are not only associated with theoretical concepts. Estonia and Chile polish the liberal growth example through market-friendly reforms that have spurred economic growth, alleviated poverty, and cultivated a vibrant private sector. After escaping from Soviet dominance, Estonia adopted low taxation, digital governance, and opened up trade. Today, it is one of the most digitalized economies in the world. [22]

These success stories depict the merits of a minimal state government model that centers on essential functions like enforcing laws and judicial contract protection while allowing private individuals to assume control over all economic activities. [23]

Implementing The Model Puerto Rico

The unincorporated Territory of Puerto Rico poses both challenges and unique prospects when advocating for economic reform. For one, adopting a libertarian view would mean prioritizing the removal of all small business and investment impediments within Puerto Rico's regulatory framework. The self-governing Puerto Rican authorities would ease the regulations governing construction, food service, and manufacturing industries in order to increase the competitive advantage of starting new business ventures within the Territory while also encouraging local industry growth.

In addition, the tax code of Puerto Rico poses a challenge that is in dire need of restructuring. The tax policies of Puerto Rico are overly complicated, lacking competitiveness, and inefficient to both individual citizens and businesses. Reducing taxes while also eliminating counterproductive subsidies and adopting taxes based on consumption will increase compliance and economic activity in the Territory.[24]

Moreover, there is a genuine urgency to restructure The Puerto Rican public sector. The Puerto Rico government has been known for its bloated bureaucracy and ineffective public services. In a bid to improve, the Puerto Rican government requires significant spending cuts, privatizing underperforming state-owned entities such as PREPA (Puerto Rico Electric Power Authority) and encouraging private participation in the education, energy, and healthcare sectors. By adopting school choice policies, parents can select schools for their children that align with their beliefs, creating a competitive market for educational quality.

The inclusion of private utility companies, along with nuclear and solar power, would greatly alleviate the failing power infrastructure on the islands while providing more dependable energy to their residents and businesses. The need for government-run services has shown the dire need for both privatization and decentralization. Puerto Rico's integration into international trade is significantly stunted by the federal Jones Act. From a Libertarian perspective, either outright abolishment or severe modification of the law is encouraged. Alternatively permitting Puerto Rico would increase competition in exports, decrease the cost of imports, and promote greater integration of the island into the international market.

Puerto Rican culture does view Libertarian principles as radical. The island's history indicates a rich ecosystem of mutual aid, community, and entrepreneurship which is key to voluntary association. Puerto Rico is able to flourish without the bureaucratic manipulation of local markets through regulation. Rather, with the implementation of policies that support such efforts, Puerto Rico would be able to thrive in innovation and self-government, rebuilding their nation on the principles of personal freedom and control.

Conclusion

Puerto Rico looks to be in a favorable situation where it can finally put its colonial history as well as its economic stagnation to rest. The borders of the island along with personal responsibility must be ascertained through free markets and its government in a libertarian outlook. The island can learn from global examples, carefully alter its local strengths, rejects dependency, and could also create a society that is both prosperous alongside honoring opportunities fulfilling liberty.

Chapter 3: Tax Reform and Entrepreneurial Incentives

The stagnant economy of Puerto Rico is experiencing painful lack of growth in part due to the convoluted and burdensome system of taxation. The combination of local and federal tax has for a long time resulted in disincentivizing entrepreneurship, repelling foreign investment, and stifling economic vitality. From a libertarian viewpoint, success hinges on the existence of unregulated economic activities, laissez faire within governance, and ready access to commerce courtesy of open-door policies. Relatively speaking, Puerto Rico must reconsider its strategies, changing island-wide taxes must replace other inefficient methods to try and spur economic growth.

The Case Proposing Simplifying of the Taxation System

Due to selective application of federal tax laws regarding Puerto Rico's territorial status, the region finds itself in an unproductive hybrid system with both local and regional levies. Since Puerto Rico has to comply with selective federal law, there is a combination of taxation and bewildering authority escalopes which create unpredictable burdens of obligations on business empresses give birth to polygon of business owners. Relatively sexy but less sophisticated models that are not specially taxed for being sexy are able to propose a different approach that eliminates bureaucracy in the form of excise taxes which simplifies the system crippled by measures of state control.

A set tax policy should have the same criteria for every individual or organization, cut back on documentation, and ensure compliance is reasonably priced. It should move from penalizing productivity to promoting reinvestment and expansion. Taxing income and corporations uniformly would remove the preference distortions and promote competition. Ultimately, a system is preferred where an entrepreneur could calculate their obligations and focus on scaling instead of getting lost in the procedural maze. The small and medium-sized businesses would also benefit from the removal of the compliance cost barrier associated with the simplified policies. The informal and long neglected portions of the economy also need life breathed into them, which makes the reduction of unnecessary licensure and bureaucratic oversight essential.

Encouraging Businesses and New Ventures

While active entrepreneurship serves as an indicator of a healthy economy, in Puerto Rico, the government is more inclined to treat it as a burden to control. Empowering entrepreneurs is best achieved through strategies that lessen regulations and provide room for innovation through strong support policies. As a result, startup-friendly environments emerge. They do suffer from minimal and predictable policies, besides fair enforcement. Investment relief is also required, alongside a fundamental change in the cultural attitude that relies heavily on state subsidies. Tax incentives directed toward certain industries or politically interested parties should be eliminated in favor of broad-based reforms. Removing barriers to entry like complicated permit procedures, inflexible labor regulations, and price ceilings will invite local entrepreneurs in addition to large scale investors. As News Is My Business highlights, strategic policy efforts need to focus on recovering dynamism in Puerto Rico's private sector, particularly in the tech, energy, and tourism industries. [25]

By far the best approach would be to create so-called 'liberty zones' across the island, where the burden of taxation and regulation is lifted significantly. These zones may spark interest from returning diaspora as well as local investors. Implementing these policies, in addition to protecting property rights and enforcing contracts, could transform Puerto Rico into a startup haven.

Stimulating Growth Through Cutting Corporate Taxes

Relatively high corporate tax rates and profit discouragements restrict the formation of capital and encourage businesses to relocate. According to libertarian theory, government action should focus on protecting markets from selective incentivization and not punishing success through heavy taxation. Hence, Puerto Rico's corporate tax structure needs a new approach – not with more exemptions, but an overall reduction to the existing rate which improves the image of the region for all types of businesses.

Puerto Rico's top corporate tax rate is 37.5% as of 2025, higher than several other US states and competing Caribbean countries. This transforms the region into an unfriendly place for manufacturing, technology, and even service-oriented businesses. If Puerto Rico reduced the corporate tax rate to a more competitive flat rate, for example 15%, the Territory could communicate strength to both international investors and local business people: growth is not only welcome here but encouraged and rewarded. [26] This reduction would fit like a glove to the federal tax regime in the event of statehood. Should Puerto Rico become the 51st state, its paradigmatic economic struggles would have to be accommodated within the US tax system's suffocating rigidity. Instead of trying to impose the same broken structures, Puerto Rico ought to pursue federal tax cubicle plans that grant legislative permission for tax experimentation within a state framework, such as federally mandated minimum tax periods, automatic spending limits, or state-controlled revenue assessments. These are consistent with libertarian governance and tried in Texas and Florida.

Concluding Remarks

Puerto Rico has until now relied on dependency models but is required to shift to empowerment innovation. The critique of a government's endeavor to overextend sustains its capability, but so does the relentless infusion of unshackled imagination waiting for a time to be unleashed. Tax cuts, and more broadly reforms restructuring taxes, are foundational—not through favoritism, but through structural-cleansing. The old Puerto Rico shudders in possibility of inventing self-perpetuating enduring harnessing.

Chapter 4: Privatization and Deregulation

The journey to prosperity in Puerto Rico requires a drastic update on how the government manages its role the economy. Shift considerations on Puerto Rico's vision for economic growth to focus primarily on the privatization and deregulation imperatives. As explained previously, these two fundamental underpinnings of privatization represent free-market ideals. libertarian economics tackle Puerto Rico's overgrown bureaucracy system its hurdles toward agility, productivity, and ample opportunities. While in the prior provided context, the government's role is imminent in guaranteeing property rights and undergirding law and order, its attempts of functioning business and micro-managing market dynamics have, more often than not, retarded economic growth and led to stagnation, rampant corruption, and resource drain.

Changing Puerto Rico's model requires a quiet but profound shift in thinking. This means letting go of the Government-owned structure of running industry whereby enabling political management is substituted with profit-minded management. This shift has become an urgent requirement for Puerto Rico due to its crippled energy sector, infrastructure debt, and eroded credit. Why? Because the dismantling of barriers controlling systems stifling entry, innovation, or competition becomes a vital necessity along with infrastructure and energy revitalization.

The Advantages of Privatization of State-Owned Businesses

Political manipulation, poor operational efficiency, and persistent financial problems has always been the nature of state owned enterprises (SOE) in Puerto Rico. The Puerto Rico Electric Power Authority (PREPA) serves as a critical example of a public monopoly which suffered through incessant blackouts, poor customer service, extreme electricity rates, and overstaffing. PREPA was already bankrupt before Hurricane Maria in 2017, but it had seriously structural problems that were exacerbated post hurricane which served to showcase the extent of issues.

Though Puerto Rico's Electric Power Authority's (PREPA) is still undergoing a transformative reform process post crippling devastation, its transmission and distribution contracts with LUMA Energy have brought it a step closer to modernization. However, the process has not been free of controversy. Critics have raised valid points of disruption to existing services, but fail to understand the gridlock systemic problems LUMA was handed over that had been ignored for decades, and actually – the time which is required to shift from such. In spite of the challenges brought from privatization, there is now an ever growing incentive and new capital targeting overall energy performance and reliability in Puerto Rico. Unchallenged political favoritism alongside free competition within a privatized set energy system has the potential to drastically reduce prices and yield high returns in the long run.

The right approach to regulation and natural monopolies, such as giving them appropriate oversight when conducting privatization, boosts productivity and customer satisfaction. Privatization in Latin America, for example, has shown to be useful in Chile and Colombia where SOEs in telecom, banking, and energy have been divested. Puerto Rico is in need of models to improve its situation, such as the privatization of the electricity sector in Chile during the 1980s which resulted in greater investment, fewer losses, and better service coverage.

Clearly marked boundaries is another factor that privatization brings to the economy. When a government is in charge of utilities or service providers, the defender of these services turns into an ally politician that doles out positions to friends. Political prizes are done away with. This encourages advanced long term planning due to the elimination of accountability. Embracing private ownership also encourages consumer demand alongside creativity and responsiveness.

Successful Deregulation: Lessons from Elsewhere

Deregulation has a critical impact on entrepreneurship, just as privatization does. In Puerto Rico, the absolute worst problem that a business owner could face is the plethora of permits, licenses, and taxes needed just to open a simple small business. From the 2021 Cato Institute report: "Local regulations, in addition to federal regulations, create an imposing atmosphere for the formation of businesses and the creation of jobs." [27]

On the other hand, Puerto Rico stands in stark contrast with economies that have embraced deregulation which showcase new business registrations, productivity, and even innovation. Lower prices as well as an increase in consumer choice followed the deregulation of the United Kingdom's transportation and energy sectors in the 1980s. In the United States, Reagan's era deregulation of air travel and trucking rode the costs lower and increased the options for services that could be used. The same steps Puerto Rico needs to take in reducing the redundant permitting systems in municipalities; easing up on the cumbersome procedures for different towns could yield similar results. Services based on the internet for licensing, inspecting, and regimented systems of taxation could greatly enhance how simple it is to operate a business. Deregulation does not mean the abdication of duty; rather, the realignment of strategy toward the bolstering of citizens through the unclogging of bureaucratic bottlenecks.

Another important focus is on labor relations. The overly protective labor policies of Puerto Rico, for instance, elicit much criticism for seeking to defend employees' interests on one hand, while on the other hand completely fail to assist with employment possibilities. Easing restrictions on the hiring and firing process, updating wage structures, and increasing the possibility of part-time work could greatly help to increase employment levels without infringing on important labor rights.

Recommendations: Sectors Ready For Reform

Puerto Rico needs to set and examine which services will benefit most from privatization and deregulation. The energy industry is one of them but there are many other equally important ones.

Transportation: Puerto Rico's public transport system is widely regarded as inadequate, underfunded, and not user-friendly. Allowing private companies to operate buses or increasing regulations on rideshare companies could enable residents to access quicker and cheaper services.

Education: There's no denying the controversial nature of this issue, but sufficed to say that the introduction of public-private educational partnerships (PPPs) have proved effective as can be illustrated by the New Orleans' case. Competition and accountability can be achieved with charter schools, school vouchers, and school choice systems.

Waste Management: Since the municipalities in Puerto Rico manage the waste at a given municipality, they do not comply with standards set for sanitation or environmental management, leading to various wastes being unsafely disposed of. Contracts or privatization of waste management services could greatly enhance service delivery and enforcement of environmental standards.

Waterworks and Sanitation Services: Most systems are antiquated and pose health risks. There is potential to improve delivery and reduce losses through regulated privatization. This model allows the private sector to operate the infrastructure under clear accountability contracts.

Tourism and the Property Market: Allow coastal regions to freely develop tourist infrastructure and lift zoning laws in order to make the most out of underused coastal property which will lead to increased employment opportunities and tax income.

Telecommunications: This sector only has partial competition and needs to be opened up, especially in rural areas. Providing tax incentives for satellite broadband coverage and faster approval processes for necessary works will serve disconnected communities.

The central recommendation is simple: do less, but do it more effectively. Create laws and regulations that defend rights, enforce contracts, and maintain a high level of clarity. All production, services, and innovations should be left to the private sector.

Although privatization and deregulation are not magic solutions, they do provide Puerto Rico with the assistance it needs to move away from dependency if carefully monitored. These tools put in place the foundations of a strong civil society. Citizens and entrepreneurs for the first time will be able to tackle issues not through political persuasion, but by using creativity and commerce.

Conclusion

Puerto Rico has suffered decades of economic stagnation due to government overreach and a dependency culture. Puerto Rico's move from dynamism to fragility requires a shift toward embracing the free market, private property ownership, and a smaller government. Prosperity can be achieved through the deregulation of state-owned monopolies and enterprise privatization. As Puerto Rico considers statehood, the island should not intend to be yet another unproductive state in the federation. Instead, Puerto Rico should strive to be a model for the rest of the country to follow by focusing on development through economic freedom while promoting constitutional civic virtue and responsibility. These reforms would not just help the people of Puerto Rico; they could help the world understand that even societies that face chronic challenges can thrive when built around free market principles of voluntary trade and individual autonomy.

Part III: The Case for Statehood

Political Equality and Representation

For over a century, Puerto Rico has existed in a peculiar political limbo—part of the United States yet not fully included in the democratic process. To this day, Puerto Ricans are still unable to vote for the president and have no congressional representation. While Puerto Ricans are citizens of the United States, they do not have the ability to vote in presidential elections, nor do they have congressional voting representatives. The absence of these democratic practices distinctly undermines the very core of the representative system as well as the libertarian notion of self governance.

The Democratic Deficit

As Puerto Rico is designated as a territory, residents do not enjoy the core liberty accompanied with political representation. Puerto Rico's political and legal status as a territory impedes citizens from exercising their right to vote or participate in the political arena. Although he or she is regarded as a congressman, the Puerto Rico Congressional Resident Commissioner, only has the house of representatives vote in committee voice vote. Puerto Rico is considered a territory of the United States. This means that Puerto Ricans can expect plenty of federally imposed laws, mandates, and economic regulations, but no House of Representative or Senate. From a libertarian perspective, there is systemic inequality which grants no political representation to the citizens governed. Such governance can only be termed as political disenfranchisement.

When people are ruled over privy to the governance system which dictates policies over him or her without his or her input, the very existence of that governance is ethically valuable and rational. In reality, governance exists, for metaphorical consideration, suffocation of Puerto Rico. This means Puerto Rico, devoid of any consent, is ruled, stifled fundamentally violates anglo american republicanism. For those who practice libertarianism should understand that enduring this sociopolitical disparity not only weakens freedoms on the other hand becomes fueled there's no other way to put it politically influenced stagnation.

The Inequity of Population Statehood

Statehood is the only remedy achievable within the framework of laws governing Puerto Rico. It would allow Puerto Rico to have two US Senators and appropriate representation in the House, regaining the voice of the people in the legislative body. Most importantly, Puerto Rico would no longer remain an overseas US territory. Maintaining US citizenship would allow for active participation in core American political processes, which is essential to shaping their future.

Historically, newly admitted states have been provided with more federal attention, infrastructure spending, and local leaders to consolidate power. For Puerto Rico, statehood is not about assimilation, but rather about protecting their unique identity while providing them the political autonomy necessary to call it self-governance. Citizens would also gain the ability to energize participation in democracy and accountability by voting for the president and actively participate in legislation at the national level.

Replacing Political Apathy with Civic Engagement

All Puerto Ricans must do is have their basic political rights granted and the Puerto Rican people would have the incentive to engage deeply in the federal political system. While local elections are ardently contested, a sense of detachment from Washington, D.C. has contributed to political apathy and cynicism. By achieving statehood, citizens will finally be able to access the levers of national power and responsibility, completely transforming the current state of disillusionment.

Increased civic participation leads to enhanced governance and increased civic responsiveness. As we have said before, representation is more than a superficial concept—it is how responsibility is executed. Such Libertarians who justify minimal government intervention paired with high individual freedoms should interpret statehood as not an addition of federal authority, but rather a division of federal influence, returning control to a people who rightfully have had such powers stripped from them.

Dignity Through Equality

Apart from the practicality, morally, the argument for statehood is based on equality and dignity. Equal treatment of citizens ought not to be withheld on the basis of a region's distance or culture in a constitutional republic. Statehood sends a message that Puerto Ricans are not second class participants in the American political experiment—but rather full-fledged ones.

Constitutional neutrality should not be perceived as political apathy, but rather active involvement to balance the scales of justice. If liberty is to be regarded as a universal value, it has to pertain to every citizen of the United States. The political independence strongly manifests itself in the failure to provide democratic representation in Congress for far too long. Statehood will put an end to this injustice and mark the beginning of the new era of widened and active inclusion.

Cato Institute notes that the Puerto Rican case should not use territorial status as 'justify claiming indefinite territory' and warrants the more political power Puerto Rico is given, the easier it can push for libertarian reforms like economic liberalization and balanced budgets which would strengthen the Puerto Rican economy and liberate them from federal oversight.[28]

Reclaiming the Republic

The constitutional principles of the United States and Puerto Rico's treatment have to come in sync. The solution to the issue is clear, either try and rule without consent or provide statehood and promised freedom. There is a compelling need for libertarians to support this development, and not just for strategic reasons—not only for why liberty requires it. Puerto Rico's current proposed status undermines the political dignity of full citizenship which every free state is entitled to. As the 51st state, Puerto Rico would have elected representatives, electoral votes and a new level of congressional esteem. A weaker citizenship dismantles ideals of the American political tradition.

Economic Benefits of Statehood

The potential economic impact of statehood on Puerto Rico is remarkable. Puerto Rico's current territorial status restricts access to certain federal programs, subjects Puerto Rico to an inequitable funding formula, and stifles Puerto Rico's long-term economic potential. On the other hand, statehood provides a gateway towards achieving parity—economic, fiscal, and structural—with the fifty states.

Gaining Access To Federal Funding Programs

Perhaps one of the most immediate advantages of statehood would be the availability of federal aid and equal funding. As a territory, Puerto Rico gets lower reimbursement levels for Medicaid, SSI, and other social programs such as SNAP in comparison to the participating states. This discrepancy fails to account for Puerto Rico's colonial status under the Insular Cases and is neither demographic nor economically rational. It is simply an outdated framework that comes along with statehood. For example, back in 2020, Puerto Rico received approximately 55% less Medicaid funding, on a per capita basis, than the average US state. This disconnect created significant underfunding of the island's healthcare infrastructure.[29] Upon becoming a state, Puerto Rico would qualify for the same formulas and safeguards as other states which could result in multi-billion dollar federal funding on a recurring basis.

Potential for Increased Infrastructure Investment

Infrastructural development is both an opportunity and a necessity for Puerto Rico. Stagnant Puerto Rican economic growth has long been due to an aging electrical grid, water system, transportation infrastructure, and insufficient economic growth on the island. Puerto Rico's status as a state would open access to a wider range of federal infrastructure funding including programs by the Department of Transportation, the Environmental Protection Agency, and FEMA, without the discretionary caps typically placed on territories. Upgrading ports, highways, and broadband access through federal funding could increase the economic competitiveness of Puerto Rico in logistics, technology, and tourism. Statehood may further promote private-public partnerships by solidifying investor confidence through guaranteed lower regulatory risk and enhanced federal support.

Advances in Credit Ratings and Investor Trust

The uncertainty surrounding Puerto Rico's legal status and limited control over its bankruptcy governance framework escalated its fiscal crisis and bankruptcy crisis until the enactment of the PROMESA Act.[30] The ambiguity would be eliminated by statehood. As a state, Puerto Rico would gain from the implicit credit guarantee associated with sovereignty at the state level which would improve credit ratings and borrowing costs. Regarding investor confidence, it would improve along with fears of political instability, statutory caps on territorial debt obligations, and investor confidence. Statehood would integrate Puerto Rico into the same legal jurisdiction as the fifty states supporting long-term investment, which could mitigate capital flight, enhance homeownership, and boost capital.

Conclusion

The fairness and functionality equilibrium serves as the backbone of the economic rationale for Puerto Rican statehood. Puerto Rico's economic challenges wouldn't be resolved with statehood, but it would grant the legal equality and tools needed to drive sustainable growth. Strengthening credit access through federal resources coupled with enhanced infrastructure investment opportunities would enable the island to leverage its newfound self-determination and work towards a prosperous future as an equal member of the American federation.

Chapter 5: Addressing Concerns and Misconceptions

For all the practical advantages and democratic benefits that Puerto Rican statehood offers, the issue remains controversial, often fueled by politically motivated misinformation, hesitation, and anxiety of a cultural nature. This chapter resolves issues of popular concern by responding to myths that have been cited by statehood opponents both in the island and in mainland America.

Myths vs. Facts Regarding the Statehood of Puerto Rico

Myth 1: Puerto Rico's culture and the Spanish language will be lost under statehood.

Debunked: New Mexico, Hawaii, Louisiana, along with other US states have retained their cultures and languages. There is no requirement for cultural assimilation in the US constitution and Spanish would still be the prominent language.

Myth 2: Puerto Ricans living in poverty will face high federal income taxes with statehood.

Debunked: The bulk of the population is below the income tax bracket. Additionally, any federal income tax that is put into place can be introduced slowly, and citizens already pay taxes through federal payroll tax (i.e. social security).

Myth 3: Puerto Rico would serve as a permanent welfare burden to the mainland United States.

Debunked: Full economic integration and increased investment would be possible with statehood which would also increase tax revenue over time. Several lower income states get more aid from the federal government than what they actually pay in taxes.

Myth 4: Puerto Rico does not wish to acquire statehood.

Debunked: The majority of voters have supported statehood in the last three plebiscites (2012, 2017, and 2020). Voter turnout and ballot design are brought up often as reasons for opposing the outcome, but the direction is undeniable.

Myth 5: Puerto Rico is unable to gain statehood due to its debt crisis.

Debunked: New York, California, and Illinois have dealt with severe fiscal crises and debt did not constitute a legal or constitutional barrier to statehood

Myth 6: Predicting partisan outcomes is speculative, and denying rights on such grounds is illegitimate.

Debunked: Puerto Rico has elected both conservative and progressive leaders claiming the population is politically diverse.

Myth 7: Puerto Rico is too small or poor to qualify as a state.

Debunked: Puerto Rico's population surpasses 20 US states, boasting a comparable or greater GDP than some. Constitutional criteria for statehood have never included size and wealth.

Myth 8: Puerto Rico must fully achieve economic self-sufficiency prior to qualifying for statehood.

Debunked: No state has ever been required an economic threshold prior to joining the union. Full access to programs and markets post statehood often stimulates economic growth.

Myth 9: Puerto Rico would demand official bilingualism or change the national language to Spanish.

Debunked: The US does not have an official language. States have the local autonomy to set language policy, and English is already widely used alongside Spanish.

Myth 10: Puerto Rico is too different culturally to be integrated as a state.

Debunked: Diversity is not a hindrance—but a key pillar of the US federal system. States already differ on religion, language, culture, ethnicity, and way of life.

Myths Of Statehood And Culture Identity

One of the strongest Puerto Rican statehood advocates, Aponte, once defined Puerto Rico as a developing country destined to become an American colony. It was Aponte's assumption that Puerto Ricans were indifferent to their dignity and destiny. In truth, their dignity and hope lie in fighting for a culture and identity that has endured active suppression for several generations and fighting fiercely against forced assimilation processes.

The Americanization theory was born in Puerto Rico during the 1950s. The fear of Puerto Rico losing its culture as a result of statehood has prevailed stubbornly for many decades. Along with frenzied arguments pertaining to statehood comes the loss, or better, the erosion of Puerto Rico's identity. Looking at American history, one instantly sees the amalgamation of a multitude of cultures under one umbrella with no nation-language required ethical. The constitution does not entail cultural or social assimilation of its constituents. On the contrary, the union's core principle is to embrace diversity, allowing each member state to preserve its national identity while promoting social integration without the burden of sacrificing its uniqueness. Also, Puerto Rican citizenship does not conflict with American identity. It is, in fact, a mark of civic pride to fight for equal rights. Statehood would not eliminate Puerto Rico's identity; rather, it would validate that its identity can exist alongside full democratic civil rights.

Explaining the Economic Consequences for Puerto Rico and the Rest of the US

One more concern has to do with the finances after statehood is granted. Detractors argue that Puerto Rico would be a fiscal liability to the US Federal Government. This argument, however, is based on a lack of understanding on budgeting and taxing at the federal level.

Although statehood would increase federal program access for Puerto Rico, it would also expand the Territory's economic output and tax base, thereby partially offsetting these costs. The majority of Puerto Ricans pay federal payroll taxes (Social Security and Medicare) and under statehood, federal income tax application would be gradual and income level indexed like the other low-income states. [31]

Puerto Rico's integration would be a slight fiscal shift compared to the entire US budget, thus, from a federal standpoint, is an insignificant change.[32] Greater formalization of labor markets and economic activity could increase fiscal revenue over time. In a looser economy, investment, entrepreneurial, and job creation would likely increase.

Political Opposition and Path Forward

Opposition to Puerto Rico's statehood comes from a myriad of political sides. Conservatives oppose Puerto Rico's statehood because they believe it would favor Democrat votes, while progressives worry about the island's conservative religious leanings. Change is also resisted for inertia—or wishful misunderstanding. Regardless, democracy should not be a balance dictated by partisan reasoning. The self-determination principle states Puerto Rico should decide their fate, not strategic electoral interests.

The way forward consists of civic education, political participation, and action from Congress. Puerto Rico has chosen statehood in several referenda votes. Now what is needed is the federal recognition and legislative action pledging to fully transition the island into statehood. This should encompass a binding plebiscite, enabling act from Congress, and a cooperative framework for Puerto Rico's structural and fiscal integration into the Union.

Conclusion

The argument against Puerto Rican statehood is grounded on fears that are out of touch with modern reality, poor economic rationale, or political maneuvering. Once armed with facts, historical context, and a respect for democratic norms, the case for statehood not only serves as a plausible argument, but one that is vital. The preservation of culture, sound financial management, and political inclusion should not be viewed as opposing concepts—they are the foundational elements of a republic united in diversity.

Cultural Self-Determination in Statehood: The New Mexico Example for Puerto Rico

Cultural Self-Determination in Statehood: The New Mexico Example for Puerto Rico

In The 51st State, we consider all the reasons people believe Puerto Rico should be welcomed as a new state, imagining what that choice could mean for the freedom and self-rule of everyone on the island. Still, one worry keeps popping up, and it is an understandable one the fear that waving a state flag would slowly wash away Puerto Ricos colorful culture, its lively Spanish, and the traditions that people on the street know by heart. That concern comes straight from a deep love for the archipelago's identity, so no one should dismiss it. Yet when we study American history from Boston to Santa Fe we see that such worries miss the point, because the United States actually grew stronger when many different cultures were allowed to speak, sing, and celebrate side by side. To show this and to argue, in a free-minded way, that statehood might even guard and boost Puerto Ricos culture, we only have to think about how New Mexico turned out.

New Mexico, kind of like Puerto Rico, has a colorful mix of traditions that grew over hundreds of years when Native people met Spanish settlers and, later on, American newcomers. Winning statehood took a long, bumpy ride because lawmakers kept debating if the new state spoke the same language, followed the same customs, and could join the union without giving up its identity. For years, leaders in Washington were nervous about admitting a place with so many Spanish speakers, strong Catholic roots, and a feel so different from the familiar eastern states because they feared it might blur the nation s image. Yet New Mexicans never gave up; they wanted the right to vote and shape their own future. When Washington finally said yes in 1912, residents walked into the union proud, knowing their local ways were not a problem to fix but a treasure worth showing off.

History has shown that those worries never came true. Today New Mexico is a colorful state where Spanish is still spoken every day and is recognized along with English as an official language. Indigenous, Hispanic, and Mexican-American customs are woven into everything people see and taste, from traditional adobe buildings and spicy dishes to glowing holiday parades. Culture not only hung on; it blossomed because neighborhoods and families had the freedom and means to care for it. Robert W. Larson puts it best in his classic book on New Mexicos statehood: New Mexicos cultural identity was not sacrificed on the altar of assimilation; instead, it became a distinctive and valued feature of its place within the nation. Statehood did not force everyone to be the same, and it brought safe government and jobs that let people keep their own ways and share them loudly with the world. [33]

To prove that something tricky can still feel personal, let's look at a curious little gem in central New Mexico called Truth or Consequences, or T or C if you want to sound like a local. Back when everybody came for the bubbling hot baths, the place proudly went by Hot Springs, but in 1950 a radio quiz show bet the town that nobody could guess its real prize, so it switched names on the air and kept the prize forever. At first, the label sounds like a cheap publicity stunt, a joke somebody else stuck on the map. Yet when you drive the winding roads in, you notice that the town has not lost itself; in fact, it greets you with vintage bathhouses, colorful pottery shops, breathtaking views of Elephant Butte Lake, and friendly folks who know the desert like family. People here laugh about the odd name but keep celebrating their healing waters and their deep ties to the arid landscape, turning the game show quip into just one more colorful thread in a much bigger story.

If a small U.S. town can swap its old title for a quirky, completely "American" name and still feel like home, why couldn't a whole archipelago like Puerto Rico keep its identity and history while becoming the fifty-first state? From a libertarian point of view, the case is even stronger. Culture isn't frozen; it lives and grows through the choices people make every day. A true libertarian government protects personal freedom and refuses to bully anyone into hiding their way of life. So when Puerto Ricans choose statehood, they aren't surrendering their heritage; they-reclaiming the right to shape their future. With full membership, they can vote in Congress and presidential races, giving them real power over federal rules. That would let them back up Spanish, support local schools, celebrate their art, and defend traditions just as loudly as any state in the union.

People living in Puerto Rico would be promised the same constitutional right as every American-to speak Spanish, honor their own holidays, play their music loud, and raise their kids in the heritage they love. Joining the Union as a state would also bring a stronger economy, and a solid economy is what keeps culture alive. Being treated as a territory has kept Puerto Rico trapped in cycles of economic uncertainty, making it hard to fund museums, pay writers and artists, or let families plan for the future. Statehood would open doors to the same federal programs the 50 states already enjoy, remove many financial barriers, and lure investors willing to stay. With money, stability, and equal status, Puerto Ricos music, stories, dance, and crafts could stop just surviving and start thriving. After all, culture does not bloom in poverty or doubt; it grows in freedom, prosperity, and the everyday choice to invest in what matters most.

To wrap it up, New Mexico's journey, told in this chapter of The 51st State, directly challenges the fear that giving Puerto Rico statehood would wipe out its culture. The story instead shows that joining the Union, especially when seen through a libertarian view, can actually hand people stronger tools to guard and even celebrate their own traditions. Puerto Rican culture is too colorful and too woven into everyday life for a change in status to wash it away. Far from shrinking, that culture would get fresh support and wider room to sparkle on both national and world stages, proving that its people, not outsiders, choose how their story is told.

Source: New Mexico, Jose Rivera 2025

Conclusion:
A Guide To Freedom And Wealth

Puerto Rico is situated at a pivot point of standstill growth and stagnation. After more than a century of incomplete citizenship and territorial status, the next steps taken should ensure growth and freedom. In this book, we have argued that statehood is not just a political option; rather, an economic and moral necessity advocating for prosperity. The promise of the American Republic, which has been a decades long aspiration, is rooted in democratic inclusion which grants eligibility for full inclusion. [34]

Summary of Key Arguments and Proposals

As earlier demonstrated, this book has laid out Puerto Rico's challenges under territorial status: scant congressional representation, limited access to federal programs, and politically-driven economic uncertainty. [35] We demonstrated how statehood would resolve these challenges by offering Puerto Rico unfettered access to federal aid and improving infrastructure creditworthiness along with investor confidence and development. [36]

We also debunked popular myths, such as fears of cultural erosion or dependency. These fears neglect the fact that historical existence and constitutional guarantees allow for great identity flexibility among states. Statehood is not a risk to Puerto Rican culture but instead presents an opportunity to fortify its preservation within a broader rights and responsibilities framework.

Action Appeal for Programmers and Citizens

The Puerto Rican population as well as US policymakers have to show courage for the next steps to go forward. For Puerto Ricans, the call is for self-determination, to demand equal rights using democratic participation and civic engagement. And as for Congress, act without delay, political calculation, but instead with integrity, vision, and decisive action. Should the people reaffirm statehood, it must be pursued through a legally-binding plebiscite, followed by an admission act to grant statehood, and a structured transition plan to implement statehood. It is not a gift to Puerto Rico, it is fulfilling the promise of constitutional equality long overdue. Imagine Puerto Rico standing on its own two feet, a shiny self-sufficient state throwing off the dust of dependency and recharging its economy. Envision freshly paved roads, bright ferry routes, and ports humming without the usual private backers from the mainland. Tourists wander beaches by day, wind farms spin quietly above, and plant-based tech labs click away in San Juan by night. Families stay put for once because good jobs, rock-solid schools, and that unmistakable Boricua spirit drive the city skylines higher while offering everyone the political respect they've been craving.

Puerto Rico possesses the human capital, adaptability, and cultural assets needed to be a fully self-sufficient and prosperous state. What is lacking is the legal framework that is needed to the Constitution so that Puerto Ricans can fully engage with the American system. This further depicts that statehood is not based on dependency, but rather on dignity, and unlocking Puerto Rico's potential becomes as the 51st star on the American flag.

Chapter 6: Civic Renewal and Institutional Reform

Puerto Rico is caught in that awful moment when the bills pile up, the headlines flash more scandal than solution, and trust flatlines. The distrust of coursing through the streets is more gut feeling than sociological footnote. Folks stare at the Capitol dome and see not a seat of public service but a stage where players trade masks while the crowd drifts away. Many stop showing up at hearings, at primaries, even at neighborhood assemblies, not out of apathy but because every try felt like re-watching a rerun with a broken remote. That slow-motion withdraw is poisonous, gnawing at the community even faster than the red tape it despises. Strip away the shiny slogans and one hard truth glows: until power is bent toward real accountability and stitched back into local lives, no banner-stamped path independence, commonwealth, statehood, or otherwise-ever brings the freedom people keep hoping for.

Recurring Scandals: The Puerto Rican Political Paradox

Puerto Rican politics has turned scandal into its own election season. Corruption flared under two party banners, Roger Rios bragged in chats, and the 2019 Ta-Ta-Gate protests roared loud enough to force Ricardo Rossello to pack his bags. Time wears on, and the audience learns to yawn. Outrage is still in the air, yet folks habitually breathe it in and hold their breath because nothing seems to change once the cameras pull away. A butterknife fix of shiny new ethics codes won't cut the rope. The island needs open books, swaggering punishments for thieves in pinstripes, and hometown councils able to fight even when the capital looks away.

Institutional Overhaul: Real Reform That Hurts (and Heals)

Nothing jolts a creature of habit like a firm set of term limits. Puerto Ricos political class spins through a tight circle of agencies, cities, and capitols, collecting titles and inside deals as if they were transit passes. The moment leaders know a clock is ticking, the cozy temptation to park themselves forever begins to fade. When permanency disappears, the lure of squeezing every last drop of public goodwill before the door closes suddenly feels risky. Reform that merely sets timetables without a hard lens on behavior misses half the point. Digital ledgers can publish procurement bids, campaign gifts, and officials net worth the same hour a deal is inked, turning rumor into record and rumor into record. Stacking that openness on a blockchain framework-star-hardened, traceable, impossible to scrub-gives voters the paperwork before the spin. The leaks may still fly, but when the files are logged in real-time, the partisan drip becomes background noise instead of the headlines main event.

Rules about how long a politician can stay in office and how openly they must act matter little unless a real price tag is attached to wrongdoing. Puerto Rico therefore needs its own slate of anti-corruption courts-run by judges who answer first to judicial ethics, not party leaders, and watched by citizen panels that know the neighborhood. Each courtroom should investigate only kickbacks, false disclosures, rigged fundraising, and similar mischief. Penalties need to be visible, severe, and melted out faster than the current crawl through bail hearings. When a governor siphons recovery money, the fallout ought to be prison, not a long-paid leave behind a desk no one else is using. Steal at that scale, and the only office left open to you should be a cell where public-leader status is formally stamped out for life.

Puerto Ricos dormant democracy has civil-society fibers that still pulse, even if they're frayed at the edges. Grass-roots alliances, pro-bono lawyers, neighborhood reporters, and seasoned non-profits have, time and again, stepped in where big government froze or faltered. If the courts supply the hard rules, these groups can supply the air: explaining, rallying, and insisting that citizens stay in the political conversation long after the evening headlines fade. Puerto Rico needs more than the usual election-time pep rally if people are to feel civics in their bones. Picture a neighborhood center that opens its doors year-round for hands-on workshops where families read first-hand excerpts of the Constitution, volunteer law students explain voting rights, and the mayor stops by-for real-to answer oddball questions. Backing could roll in from state universities or willing small businesses that sign off on keeping the space neutral, so no party gets to claim the stage forever.

Politicians wobble, policies stall, yet the idea of democracy keeps breathing on the streets if citizens refuse to let it sink. When Maria knocked out the red tape, barber shops and church basements handed out food and maps; those same networks can now turn out town-hall debates or protest signs faster than a tweet. Grassroots volunteers, not press releases, become the immune system the system never knew it needed. Handing neighborhood councils clear budgets and real say-so is like planting sunlight in the barrios. Talk of statehood or any big political fix must start by putting power as close as possible to the doorsteps where decisions land, a principle fancy experts label subsidiarity. Decisions that drip downward lose punch, but choices born in barrio meetings bounce back up with respect. The trick is letting that loop happen again and again until local voices expect their ideas to stick.

Reinvesting in city halls means treating mayors and municipal governments as more than figureheads or ribbon-cutting guests. Real power-flowing from zoning codes to school boards to everyday policing should rest in local hands as long as civil liberties and the constitution keep watch. Budget freedom needs real teeth, so any state order must come with money that matches the mandate. Picture this: a jury of neighbors gathered in a gym, deciding on sidewalks or parks by scribbling yes or no on a colored slip. Programs like that, seen in places from Porto Alegre to Paris, turn dusty spreadsheets into shared choices and help citizens feel they spotted government instead of the other way around.

Statehood for Puerto Rico gets the loudest cheers in this book, mostly for closing the political inequality gap and locking in federal rights. Sure, two new senators, five electoral votes, and a flow of dollars look good on paper, yet without home-grown fixes the island could end up a smaller carbon copy of its old self-just with bigger headlines. Civic renewal, Puerto Ricos residents often say, isn't a precondition for statehood; it's the moral wind at that states back. Should the island finally join the Union as its fifty-first star, the admission papers ought to tell a story of resilience-painting colonial neglect as the backdrop and public grit as the foreground. [37]

The Long Haul of Liberty

No one signs up for the glamor of civic repair, and most institutional fixes never arrive on a deadline. In Puerto Rico, however, such tedium has become a question of staying alive. The people have survived the empire, economic crash, and off-island indifference; what they cannot outlive is the silence of everyone who could still lend an ear. Puerto Rican freedom, if it means anything at all, must first echo through the schoolyards of Carolina, the plazas of Ponce, and the barrios of Bayamon.

A freer island lives or dies by the scattering of power, the shaming of corruption, and the waking-up of neighborhood responsibility. Those points arent bumper-sticker lingo; they are lifelines for a people too dignified to be ordered around and too clear-eyed to be bribed.

The Department of Justice took the unusual step of sharing its Puerto Rico findings in a mid-summer 2019 release. Those notes were indexed under Public Corruption in Puerto Rico and now rest in the agency's archived newsroom.

Chapter 7: Education, Human Capital, and Self-Reliance

Puerto Ricos public schools fall into the same tired groove every dawn, a schedule that feels more museum exhibit than modern classroom. Rigid age brackets march kids along conveyor belts, yet the diplomas too often arrive accompanied by worrying skill gaps. In 2024 the NAEP math snapshot put the islands pupils at 184, a full 53 points-and five grades-below the American mean of 237. [38] Parents bent on brighter outcomes should not be handed another cookie-cutter program; they need fresh options that fit an economy where nimble knowledge makes the difference.

School Choice: Vouchers and Charters

Vouchers and charter schools have started to dot Puerto Ricos educational landscape, yet the effort stutters across municipal boundaries and shifting regulations. [39] Even so, nearly 350,000 learners nationwide, including those on the archipelago, now depend on private vouchers or tax-credit pathways, according to Ed Choice. Thirty-one states, D.C., and the Commonwealth itself embed some flavor of state-backed choice within their laws. Studies compiled in a Harvard-reviewed meta-analysis show that public campuses facing the spur of private competition gain between two and four percentage points in reading and math, numbers that, while modest, can tip a test score from failing to passing.

A tight study by the National Bureau of Economic Research says that when charters bump into the regular school system, they lift low-income kids reading scores as if they had an extra eight school days each year. Puerto Rico, where classrooms often trudge along without urgent improvement, could meet that boost by letting more schools compete for students instead of settling for the status quo. If lawmakers attach clear rules-regular report cards, real performance benchmarks, fair funding-sharing-voucher programs rarely push children into separate, unequal corners; usually, families just feel happier and learn more.

Plenty of parents prefer to steer the ship themselves, and co-ops let them do that while still mixing in other people's expertise. Across the island a learning cluster might hold a science fair in one patio, run a coding camp in another, and roast pineapples over a backyard fire for a story-writing splash. Getting to Puerto Rico there isn't expensive, since old regulations keep tripping families up for no good reason. If the government eases the red tape but makes sure every child is tested now and then, micro-schools, bilingual design workshops, and Saturday inventors' labs can spring up almost overnight. Parents gain real control, neighborhoods start pooling talent, and kids pick up skills that employers actually mention in job ads.

Pipeline to Prosperity: STEM, Entrepreneurship, Civic Literacy

In today's mesh of markets, a grounding in science, tech, engineering, or math keeps upward mobility within reach. A tight 2018 survey from Union College tracked states where STEM training coincided with sharper output in factories and software shops. Nationally, nearly 69 cents of every GDP dollar drips from STEM hands, and those workers take home roughly two paychecks for every one printed outside the field. [40]

Against that backdrop, classrooms in Puerto Rico could flip their scripts. Picture seniors coding a weather app before the first bell, puzzling out a server crash by supper, and selling a side hustle to a local shop owner before curfew. Workbenches stacked with Arduinos, 3-D printers, and auto-provisioned cloud space would churn out new makers the way factories once churned out widgets. Entrepreneurship can tag along for the ride. A short course in balance sheets, a longer stretch practicing a pitch, and suddenly students are thinking payroll instead of pop quizzes. They step into the world either ready to clock gig hours or bold enough to incorporate before the ink dries on their diplomas.

Civic know-how can't be an afterthought. Young people who can balance a household budget should also know how to grill a council member. Weekly exercises- mock town halls, policy bake-offs, fake legislature votes-give the abstract concept of democracy a muscular workout in real time. The goal is simple: citizens who show up question what they're told, and know that authority can be a temporary job description.

Early Investment in Human Capital

Economists keep circling back to preschool, calling it the place where spending pays off most. Long-term research by James Heckman, the Nobel laureate you probably heard about, shows families save on health care and courts when kids blast off academically in their first years. Think of Puerto Rico: stronger, high-quality pre-k classes dont drain the budget, they mine the future for taxpayers and entrepreneurs. For families pinch-tight on cash, a solid early program flips the script and sets a steady learning beat that lasts a lifetime.

Policy Strategy and Recommendations

A new education playbook for Puerto Rico could lay out steps that feel ambitious yet doable. One chunk says let choice ripple wider. Vouchers do heavy lifting in forgotten barrios, while clear charter rules keep watchdogs awake. Grab ideas from U.S. Ed Choice programs, and don't forget to remix them for Boricua neighborhoods. [41] Triple that impulse by unbuttoning the homeschooling rules. Trim red tape but ask parents to show progress once a year, then watch STEM co-ops and bilingual groups blossom.

Next, pile on real-life science action. Team up with local unis, nonprofits, and even the cell-phone factory down the road to drop labs, mentors, and hands-on boot camps right in the hallways. A pilot tech-charter that runs on startup energy could even lure the coders we keep reading about in Twitter threads. Finish the map with civic engine rooms: weekly modules on budgets, mock trial runs, and the soap-opera pace of lawmaking that land in high-school schedules as reliably as math.

Seed early education. Public and private backers can layer their dollars, but they must target low-income neighborhoods and follow the money with tough reports on who's reading, who's writing, and who's counting profitably.

Puerto Rico can flip from waiting for help to standing on its own if classrooms start turning out readers and tinkerers instead of empty folders. A single third-grader who masters the alphabet today may be opening a co-op tomorrow, and the neighborhood that teaches civics well can end up in charge of its own council. Statehood or an upgraded commonwealth status might be on the ballot soon, yet real freedom shows up first in classrooms rich with choices, in internships that link students to living wages, and in Puerto Ricans who know their rights as well as their duties. Investing in education that prizes liberty is, at heart, investing in a future where Islanders steer their own values, their own skills, and yes, their own territory.

Chapter 8: Building the 51st State: A Strategic Roadmap

Moving Puerto Rico from territory to statehood can't be a headline that fades in a week. It has to sit in the daylight long enough for Congress-and the public-to feel it in their bones. Nailing down a mechanics-heavy road map, complete with whiteboards full of dates and dollar signs, is the only way the next vote doesn't turn into another shrug. Kind of like seeing a pothole finally get filled instead of just painted over year after year.

One from Plebiscite to Pressure

Take the Puerto Rico Status Act that landed in Washington in 2023 (S. 3231/ H.R. 2757). [42]The proposal lines up a federally financed ballot for November 2, 2025, listing statehood, independence, and free association right at the top. If none of those choices cross the majority finish line, a runoff steps in. Sticklers read that as a neat, authorized highway sign rather than the usual fork in the road. Congress still has to keep the engine running after the ink dries, which is the giant, noisy caveat nobody can afford to overlook.

A ballot outcome, even if it rings in favor of statehood, is really the opening act. Birds-eye support only counts if the voters, plus the five-million-plus Puerto Ricans living elsewhere, keep banging on doors until the briefcase-wavers on Capitol Hill finally stand up. Picture an unbroken wave of phone calls, letters, and downright stubborn visits; the kind of ruckus Congress learns to dread in a good way. Turn that energy loose, and the odds tip from hopeful to doable.

Grassroots Engines that Move Congress

- Pipes and posts alone don't build statehood. Yard-by-yard coalition work, almost campaign-like, gives lawmakers something they can feel.
- Door-to-door crews fan out across barrios, college blocks, old towns. Volunteers train one night, hit the streets the next, turning small talk into new signatures and fresh registrations.

- Phone banks light up after sunset, buzzing from Florida to New York. A quick how-to-vote text makes the distant feel local, captures nods that add up fast.

- Strange bedfellows can shock a room. PIP, the Civic Victory crew, even a handful of GOP folks side-by-side show Washington the ask isn't coming from nowhere.

- Swing states own the calendar. When their reps hear about Jefferson, Miami, and Harrisburg screaming the same thing, ignoring the pile of petitions feels wrong.

Sketching Tomorrow Before the Ink Dries

- Statehood clicks the moment a working government handbook is waiting on the chair. A Proposed Puerto Rico State Constitution written upfront dodges the drift most territories stumble into.

- Budget caps sit at the top. No spending vice grips, no surprise tax spikes-every mayor knows the ceiling before the first dollar lands.

- Term limits get an early stamp, and transparency clauses repeat like a chorus. Lessons from past muck-ups earn their place twice, just to be sure.

- Municipalities get room to breathe. Each town decides what fits so long as subsidiarity keeps the center from swallowing the edges.

- A concrete implementation plan, complete with budgets and agency checklists, gives wary lawmakers and skeptical voters something they can hold in their hands. It turns statehood from a promise into a project that looks ready to move the morning after the last vote.

- When uncertainty lingers, every attempt to make progress seems to stall. Milestones laid out in public help keep the momentum going, and the calendar soon fills with told-you-so deadlines.

Certification of the result within thirty days.

- Delivery of those certified results to Congress and a freshly inked admission act on the House floor within sixty.
- Senate hearings, a committee mark-up, maybe a few late-night phone calls, then a final floor vote inside a hundred eighty days.
- One pen stroke from the President, and the new state is in the Union before Thanksgiving.
- That clock-watching pace gets tracked on dashboards, text alerts, and wall posters in community centers, so no one can say they missed it when the dates slip by.

Binding referenda carry real weight only when both the island elite and their metropolitan counterparts promise to live by the outcome. That was New Caledonia's breakthrough, proof that clarity of intent can beat decades of half-hearted votes.[43] Puerto Rico, by contrast, has collected nonbinding tallies like trophies, and all they proved was how easy it is to ignore the public.

To turn the 2025 ballot into a true binding moment, Washington sponsors have to sign on early and speak in unison, so the public hears them before the first booth opens. Advocacy groups-LULAC, the US Hispanic Chamber, key organizations in the Puerto Rican diaspora-have to issue joint statements during the campaign, praising the vote and saying they'll treat the result as final, no wiggle room.[44]

Congressional hearings gain a bit more weight when independent eyes are watching eyes like those of retired Supreme Court justices or respected constitutional scholars. Their presence turns what is often a partisan stage into something that looks, at least on the surface, like a courtroom in search of facts. A shared stamp of legitimacy from such figures can make the eventual plebiscite more than a poll; it turns the result into a plausible bulwark against future legal challenges, giving it a shelf-life that public opinion alone does not supply.

Even after a shiny new statehood bill clears Congress, the real test arrives during the messy hand-off. Opponents, emboldened by loopholes, can tie the process in knots with lawsuits, funny-money reinterpretations of census data, or phantom constitutional concerns that somehow pop up overnight. To blunt that stall, political leaders should quietly promise the basic tools: dollars for transition offices and automatic switches so Social Security, Medicaid, and other federal lifelines talk to the island as a State instead of a territory. A bi-national commission, half from the island and half from the mainland, then meets every month or every week at first-to track deadlines, unstick bottlenecks, and argue over whether unforeseen problems really are unforeseen. Sunset clauses tucked into the law can flip the deal from temporary to permanent on a fixed date, closing off Congressional chances to sleep on the vote forever.

What happens when the wind suddenly loses its punch? Shifts in mainland politics, fresh economic woes on the island, or bigger headlines grabbing Capitol Hills' attention can yank the carpet out from under quick momentum. Organizers can light warning flares weeks ahead of key dates, flooding social media with messages that double as fire drills. Columns, blogs, and diaspora press pieces then frame any slowdown not as caution but as a democracy on pause, a failure voters did not ask for. If all else stalls, nonprofit legal squads are already strapped, ready to file the first suit, waving the binding constitutional language that Washington wrote for itself. Every proposed backup safeguard turns statehood into something more than spirit and ink; it pushes the idea toward complex law and indelible politics.

Conclusion

Crafting the fifty-first star on the flag goes well beyond collecting votes in a ballroom. It hinges on brilliant timing, relentless pressure, clear messaging, and a stubborn refusal to back down. Sightable milestones stir public energy, and that same energy gives legislators the cover they need to act. If the blueprint is followed, what begins as minimum-viable politics could blossom into a bipartisan juggernaut event local history classes will not forget.

Chapter 9:
Support for Statehood - Puerto Ricos Referendums

Puerto Rico's long walk toward statehood has stretched through one popular vote after another, each ballot reflecting changing opinion and a deepening call for equal treatment. From the archipelago's first plebiscite in 1967 right up to the planned vote in 2024, support for turning Puerto Rico into the fifty-first state has mostly moved upward, even when arguments grew loud and politics tangled. These ballots, although only advisory, still show how many Puerto Ricans think about their place in America, how they picture their rights, and how they want the archipelago's identity to fit with the flag that flies overhead.

1. 1967: Beginning the Conversation

On July 23, 1967, Puerto Rico asked its people to speak directly and kicked off a series of votes still going today. Voters had Three Roads in front of them: stay as a Commonwealth, become a State, or walk toward full Independence. Back then, nearly 60.4 percent chose to keep Commonwealth status, while 38.8 percent said Yes to Statehood.[45] Even so, that strong minority pushed leaders to keep talking about what it would actually mean to merge the island fully with the United States.

2. 1993-1998: Rising Hopes, Then Let-Down

In a second island-wide vote held in 1993, nearly half the public-48.9 percent-chose to keep the commonwealth while 46.6 percent leaned toward statehood, leaving the outcome razor thin. The close gap proved that many citizens were pausing to reconsider exactly how they wanted the future to shape the archipelago. Fast-forward to 1998 and the trend deepened; yet again no option crossed the magic fifty-point mark still, statehood earned 46.6 percent by itself, breaking away from backers of independence and commonwealth. More Puerto Ricans seemed ready to try change at long last, even if one answer still could not pull the whole island together. [46]

3.2012: Statehood Gets a Clear Majority

The 2012 vote changed the game for Puerto Rico. Instead of listing every idea under the sun, lawmakers set up two simple questions: first, should the island keep its current status, and second, what future do you prefer-independence or statehood. [47] When people answered that second question, an eye-popping 61.2 percent picked statehood, the biggest share ever. Because the vote had no legal weight, critics brushed it aside, but it still stands as the clearest public thumbs-up for full U.S. statehood the island has shown. [48]

4. 2017 and 2020: Continued Momentum

The 2017 plebiscite delivered a wild figure: 97 percent of those who bothered to vote said yes to statehood. Yet only one-quarter of registered voters actually showed up, since many commonwealth fans stayed home. Critics quickly jumped in, insisting that real democracy needs big turnout, not just a big number. Two years later, the 2020 ballot also showed statehood on top at 52.5 percent, but close to 47.5 percent said no, making the race tighter than ever. Compared to earlier decades, the larger turnout and closer split prove more Puerto Ricans are finally thinking hard about these choices, even if they disagree. [49]

5. 2024: Continued Growth for Statehood Support

Come Election Day, November 5, 2024, Puerto Ricans found three clear paths on their ballot-statehood, independence, or a freely associated republic-and the old colonial commonwealth option was gone. About 58.6 percent chose statehood this time, while 29.6 percent still wanted independence and just 11.8 percent leaned toward free association. Because statehood has won the last four votes in a row, this latest result once more shows the islands steady drift toward equal standing with the mainland. [50]

Look back sixty years and you'll see a gradual pull toward statehood, starting at only 38.8 percent in 1967, when the commonwealth still dominated, and rising to 58.6 percent today. That clear upward curve suggests a broadening agreement about where Puerto Rico wants to go.

Residents are weighing statehood for down-to-earth reasons; changing identities, new generations coming of age, and everyday concerns like federal aid, disaster relief, and stable job issues that play out very differently for a territory.

Local politics mirror that moves, as statehood-seeking groups, especially the Partido Nuevo Progresista, keep the question in the spotlight and push it front and center at every election.

6. Limitations and Congressional Reality

Yet, we have to admit something awkward: the votes on Puerto Ricos future have no real power on their own. Congress controls the final say, and so far it has walked the fence instead of picking a clear road. Critics remind us that earlier plebiscites also came with bumps. The 1998 ballot slipped in a fuzzy none-of-the-above option that tangled the meaning. A decade later, a major boycott and thin turnout drained trust from that count. Previewing 2024, some say the question cuts out commonwealth and wears a party logo. Even with those problems, the steady tilt toward statehood shows many islanders are just worn out waiting for full rights.

7. Towards the Future

The steady yes for statehood from Puerto Ricos people carries real moral punch, but without Congress acting that yes becomes mostly a symbolic gesture. Today the island stands at a crossroads in its democracy: more voters than ever want statehood, yet the final call sleeps in a federal chamber that moves with glacial rhythm. The next goal is simple but tough-turn that growing public energy into real hustle on Capitol Hill.

After decades of voting, Puerto Ricos referendums are no longer just count-the-nose exercises; they now echo with a raw, steady plea for the same rights Americans enjoy on the mainland, and ask Congress to stop looking the other way.

Chapter 10: Libertarian Political Platform for Puerto Rico

A Vision of Liberty and Government of Minimal Intervention with Economic Freedom

Foundational Principles

This is perhaps the most pivotal moment in Puerto Rico's history. This platform outlines a bold, liberty-focused framework designed to achieve the self-determined, prosperous future Puerto Rico deserves. It aims to provide rooted an Puerto Rico is not directed by bureaucrats, but rather, by the innovation, industry, and moral self-determination of its inhabitants.

I. Reform of the Executive Branch

Reorganizing Government to Function as a Servant rather than a Master

A. Shrinking and Streamlining

Eliminate duplicate services and agencies through parallel audits of all executive departments.

Create agencies with measurable outcomes that are public value or constitutionally legitimate.

Limitations on all created agencies to prevent nepotism and the infiltration of appointees into the administration.

B. Spending Restraint

Institute measures that ensure any spending resulted from new programs to have an equal value cut from other areas.

Implemented every single peso must justify its previous year's expenditures.

Reject federal funding that comes with free market or constitutional rights violations.

C. Decentralization and Local Empowerment

Restore core decision-making power to municipalities, particularly in the areas of education, health, and infrastructure.

Substitute local referenda for top-down executive orders where applicable, reaffirming the subsidiarity principle.

D. Ending Economic Cronyism

Remove government contracts, grants, or subsidies to firms with political connections.

Prohibit executive branch intervention in competition among private sector markets.

II. Legislative Branch Reform

Restoration of the Rule of Law and Individual Sovereignty

A. Lawmaking With Restraint

Implement a "One-In, Three-Out" strategy by suggesting that for every new legislation passed, three redundant regulations must be revoked.

Require a Constitutional Compatibility Statement for all proposed bills to avoid unlawful overreach.

Implement a Sunset Law requiring all non-essential laws to automatically expire after ten years unless renewed.

B. Tax and Economic Strategy

Simplify the taxation system by replacing the multi-tiered income taxation system with a flat or consumption tax that encourages work and savings.

Remove corporate taxes that stifle innovation. competition lowers costs, consumers benefit.

Remove tax-privileges that facilitate corruption or manipulation.

C. Decriminalization and Civil Liberties

Legalize cannabis completely and take a harm reduction approach to non-violent personal behaviors, decriminalizing them.

Advocate for gun ownership rights while opposing amendments that breach the Second Amendment.

Honor bodily autonomy by protecting legal boundaries for sexuality, medicine, and life contracts for informed adults.

D. Openness and Public Involvement

Mandate unrestricted digital access to all legislative sessions, records, and votes for the public.

Mandate stringent conflict-of-interest declarations for all legislators and their families.

Enable citizens to directly repeal laws through referendum-trigger mechanisms.

III. Restructuring the Judicial Branch

The Enablers of Tyranny, Not Guardians of Liberty

A. Preservation and Independence of the Judiciary

Assign judges non-renewable fixed terms to lessen political ties and streamline impartiality.

Judicially-bound Puerto Rican and US Constitutions must be interpreted with originalism to curb judicial overreach and legislative replacement.

Create an ethics tribunal with citizen participation to handle complaints of judicial misconduct.

B. Reforming the Criminal Justice System

Civil asset forfeiture may only occur after due process and conviction.

Non-violent offenders must be released on bail to eliminate socio-economic discrimination.

Change arbitrary state penalties to the means of punishment aimed at compensation to victims.

C. Access to Legal Services

Set up civil dispute arbitration courts at lower costs to discourage protracted legal battles.

Respecting Puerto Rico's bilingualism, all court proceedings and documentation should be available in Spanish and English.

Defining a jury bill of rights to guarantee informed and empowered participation of citizens in the justice process.

Cross-Branch Strategic Initiatives

Integrating Governance with Liberty

Privatization: Government relinquishes ownership of utilities, the public transportation sector, and media outlets. These are now entrusted to private, competitively regulated providers that operate without governmental bias.

Education Reform: Issues universal education ESAs, allowing parents to unlock funds and utilize them in private, charter or homeschool options.

Anti-Corruption Initiative: Prohibits all lobbying by government contractors and imposes real-time transparency for public contracts, enforcement of stringent consequences for public fund abuse.

Blockchain Governance: Integrated land registries, public budgets, and voting systems on blockchain to curb corruption and bolster citizen trust.

New Constitution: Citizens convene a constitutional convention that integrates these principles into a charter grounded in natural law and classical liberalism.

Conclusion: Puerto Rico, Finally Free

A Puerto Rico libertarian is not characterized by government provisions but by the absence of government overreach. Puerto Rico: A bold call to liberate us from explosive government overreach, and in turn, what works—freedom, markets, and personal accountability. Puerto Rico is positioned to take the lead not as a dependent state or Territory, but as a dynamic, self-reliant, creatively empowered, and economically flourishing star in the American constellation.

Chapter 11: Where Libertarianism Has Worked

Libertarianism tends to sound tidy on paper-keeping the state lean, letting markets roam, and treating personal choice as the guiding star. In the wild, though, its playbook is sprinkled here and there, rarely painted in bright, unbroken strokes. Still, some places show what happens when policy-makers step back and let citizens get on with it. Their leaps forward prove that just enough restraint, when mixed with an appetite for risk, can flip the script on wealth and welfare.

1. Hong Kong: The Laissez-Faire Powerhouse

Early in the 1800s, British traders spotted a sleepy harbor and turned it overnight into a tax-haven aquarium where money moved in and out with almost no strings. Sir John Cowperthwaite ran the place with a stubborn refusal to fuss over figures-in fact, he kept the GDP ticker off because, he said, it would only tempt officials to meddle more.[51] Flat income at 15 percent, zero capital gains, zero sales taxes, and an economy that almost begged foreign firms to unpack and stay put. Some folks call this recipe minimalism; the city, thanks to those rules, ended up earning the nickname success by saturation. [52]

Economic Outcomes

Between 1965 and 1989, Hong Kong raced ahead, its GDP-per-head leaping at an average of roughly 6.5 per cent each twelve months. By the late 1980s that figure had pulled the territory even past the United Kingdom. The Fraser Institute kept waving its red-and-white banner, awarding the colony first place in economic freedom year after year. Tight control over taxes, lean public debt, well-sheltered property rights, and nearly free-flowing trade left the government very much in the background. [53]

Entrepreneurs thrived on that openness. Many glide outright into global markets the moment they register a modest shop sign in Mong Kok. Financiers, exchange dealers, and shipping tycoons, attracted by the easy rules, pushed the citys lights into the countdowns that now keep the world awake.

Limits and Caveats

Hong Kongs golden story has always stayed fenced beside its blemishes. Ownership of sprawling plots-including stretches close to the runway-clearly belongs to a select dozen families, and rent bills speak louder than any headline growth. Surveys chronicle a widening gap, counting the shin-honeyed suits in Central and the five-floor walk-ups that swell at the border. Some policy insiders argue the tangle of advice, exemption clauses, and off-record bargaining smells more like cronyism than unchained capitalism.

In the long run, markets lean on the beams of law as much as trade masts rely on tarpaulins. Once judges proved less independent and the 2020 National Security Law parked free-speech umbrellas, that balance tipped severely. Prosperity, it turns out, thrives on civil breathing space-even if compacted back to a narrow original libertarian draft. [54]

1. Estonia: The Digital Libertarian Playground

Background & Liberal Reform

When the Soviet Union broke apart, a new Estonian spirit refused to linger in the past. Lawmakers smashed the old state monopolies, handed factories to private hands, and worked late into the night on a rule-of-law code they could actually read.[55]

Bold flat taxes, lean budgets, and plenty of fiber-optic cable soon followed. Digital IDs, e-governance portals, and internet auctions made the country feel almost virtual before most of Europe had broadband.

Economic and Social Outcomes

Fast-forward twenty-five years and Estonia has outpaced several ex-Soviet neighbors, its skyline dotted with the logos of home-grown start-ups. Per-capita GDP now sits well above the EU average, and foreign investors treat Tallinn like an open door.

Global watchdogs rank the country in the top ten for economic freedom, its finances steady and its tax schedule leveled off at 20 percent for both firms and people. Tax receipts come in, spending stays disciplined, and the digital legal system keeps the books visible to everyone.

Limits and Caveats

The lightning pace of change shocked some workers, and a few critics warn that an all-digital state could swivel into a surveillance state if the right guardrails disappear. Estonia proves that a nimble government can turbo-charge growth, yet that same machine needs constant human eyes.

Why These Cases Matter for Puerto Rico

1. Government Size & Predictability

A lean, rule-bound public apparatus, as seen in both Hong Kong and Estonia, can surprise everyone by turbo-charging growth.

2. Rule of Law & Institutional Integrity

People keep investing only when courts stay fair, regulations stay clear, and property claims stay safe. Take those guards away, and freedom itself slides.

3. Harnessing Crisis Opportunity

Estonia jumped on reform the second the Soviet Union collapsed, turning shock into lasting renewal. Puerto Rico will probably get a similar, messy opening after bankruptcy or a blackout-if it moves fast.

4. Tension Between Economic & Civil Freedoms

Hong Kongs faltering political freedoms prove that fat wallets don't guarantee open debate. A truly free society needs both money and voice in working order.

5. Pragmatism over Purity

Neither Estonia nor Hong Kong is a textbook libertarian, yet each mixes core libertarian ideas-trade, deregulation, ironclad property rights-with enough democracy to keep citizens in the game. Puerto Rico can steal that playbook without serving the ideology raw.

Policy Implications for Puerto Rico

Rewrite the tax code to trim rates, clear loopholes, and kill any red tape that stops new businesses from opening tomorrow.

Regulate, Don't Control

The government can step back without vanishing. Handovers work; independent watchdogs, private firms, and market signals keep the lights on in Hong Kong and Estonia.

Strengthening Legal Institutions

Solid property titles matter more than glossy maps. Quick courts and painful anti-corruption teeth turn fragile promises into real confidence.

Use Crisis Momentum

Estonia rebuilt in the wake of war and chaos; Puerto Rico sits on a debt crater. Pulling reforms through the storm is ugly, but staying quiet is uglier still.

Maintain Civil Freedoms

Growth can be loud, yet personal freedoms should never be background noise. Hong Kongs recent woes remind the world of that fragile balance.

Conclusion

Pure libertarianism may be a myth, yet the core ideas sparking prosperity in Hong Kong and Estonia stay vivid. Minimal red tape, maximum accountability, and a hopeful bite of democracy gave room for people to invent and invest.

Puerto Rico finds itself at the dispatching point. By borrowing those lessons and fastening overdue fixes, it could leap from survival mode to genuine economic flight. The voyage will hurt-skeptics will shout, storms will grin-but the epochal risk is still smaller than choosing stagnation. History whispers that real liberty, patently applied, keeps doors flung open.

The Honorable Officials of Puerto Rico and Their Colleagues in the United States Congress

A Call for Bold Action on Puerto Ricos Future For Liberty, Prosperity, and Mutual Benefit

Greetings, Public Servants,

Puerto Rico wakes up every morning with energy enough to power the Caribbean, yet the island still drags around an outdated political backpack. Too many rules and too little runway mean books, goods, and bright ideas often stall long before they reach the marketplace. That reality may look local on the map, but the ripple touches taxpayers and voters from Fordham Road to Fort Worth. Fixing it will require the kind of American courage most people only read about in the history section.

Coordinated action, long promised and too rarely delivered-is now a must-have, not a nice-to-have. Joining forces across the Capitol and La Fortaleza could mean anything from streamlined oversight to full-blown statehood. What matters is that the blueprint be clear, liberty-minded, and centered on individual rights, fair markets, and a brand of government that stays accountable long after the cameras leave.

Puerto Rico is edging toward a turn in the road that, if handled right, could rev up business like nowhere else in the Caribbean. Its morning sun already shines over a people who blend old-world warmth with new-world smarts, and the island has room to play with tax rates, labor rules, and what it means to govern.

Picture this place in five years: a coder files an app and waits hours, not months, for a permit. Teachers open a school at the corner cafe-and competition drives them all to get better, faster. Paychecks stay light on deductions, so every late night and long weekend shows up in the checkbook.

None of that is a daydream. Estonia attracted talent with e-residency and clever digital laws; Singapore stitched open trade to tight discipline and boomed. Puerto Rico can borrow the best bits and still feel like Puerto Rico, not a themed pop-up.

A freight train of fresh capital would streak in, and the United States would hold the ticket. The mainland gets a bilingual workforce, a bulwark against bad actors in the Caribbean, and living proof that federalism can stretch without snapping. The islands comeback, in short, serve the republic as much as its own people.

People on the island say, again and again, that real power comes from liberty, not a parade of bureaucratic orders draped in good intentions. Turning that belief into practice would send a simple, stubborn message: we still trust ordinary men and women to run their own lives.

What Needs to Happen Now

Congress should stop circling the issue and nail down a calendar for settling Puerto Ricos political future. Statehood, independence, or something in between- once the voters decide, the rest of the country must honor the verdict and get to work, not file away another toothless report.

The island is buried in relic rules that slow production and punish risk-taking. A fresh tax code, paired with a clean swipe at federal strings that don't fit its size, could turn idle energy into payrolls almost overnight.

Real authority ought to flow downhill, not get stuck in San Juan the way traffic does at rush hour. Neighborhood councils and citizen-run budgets could finally show people that government is a tool, not the whole toolbox.

Design a handful of Free Enterprise Zones where red tape fades, capital-gains levies vanish, and contracts are worth the paper they're printed on. That combination would lure outside investors while giving home-grown start-ups the runway they need to grow.

Charter schools, cooperatives, and renegade homeschool families deserve elbow room, not a maze of permits and inspections. Real educational freedom allows parents, teachers, and students to tinker until something works for everybody.

Liberty does not arrive on the back of a government check; it steps forward, dirty boots and all, when people are given responsibility instead of handouts.

Puerto Rico does not need another headline-grabbing bailout; the island needs breathing space. Clearer boundaries, surer rules, and space to compete will do far more good than another lopsided infusion of cash.

History shows that when Puerto Ricans have real freedom, they stitch together families, start ventures, and build communities that last. Yet red tape and honking promises too often smother that spark before it can catch.

Elected leaders in San Juan and Washington, the moment for action is already overdue. Every year that passes without change, we bleed talent, freeze investment, and invite unrest; put differently, the price of inaction keeps compounding.

Bold reforms can turn Puerto Rico into a living, breathing poster child for what liberty can deliver-and the message would echo well beyond the Caribbean.

Respectfully,

Jose Rivera

Puerto Rican and Advocate for Free-Market Pro-Statehood Reform

Guest Collaboration

Political Status and Economic Liberty: A Libertarian View on Puerto Rico's Labyrinth

By Diego H. Cadenas

Source: Diego H. Cadenas Dall-E 2025

Introduction

From a libertarian perspective, Puerto Rico's political condition is less a matter of status and more a reflection of structural stagnation. The island's political debate remains stuck between nostalgia, dependency, and slogans, while vital institutional reforms are postponed indefinitely. This chapter explores Puerto Rico's long-standing status dilemma through a different lens: one that prioritizes liberty, responsibility, and institutional strength over political identity. The goal is not to endorse or reject a status formula, but to ask a deeper question—what kind of country do we want to build, and under what conditions could that country be truly free?

1. The Broken Status Quo

Puerto Rico's current status is neither stable nor transitional. It is an indefinite suspension of democratic will, overseen by a territorial clause that gives Congress full authority over the island. Despite its American citizenship, Puerto Rico lacks full representation, voting rights in presidential elections, and equal treatment under key federal programs. Meanwhile, a fiscal control board—appointed by Washington—oversees much of the island's budget and policy, reducing local self-rule. Rather than confronting this contradiction, political parties have learned to manage it. The result is a form of colonial inertia: a place that governs itself just enough to delay change, but not enough to solve its structural problems.

2. The Referendum Trap

Puerto Rico has held six status referenda since 1967. In 1993, the ELA won by a narrow margin. In 1998, most voters chose "none of the above." In 2012, a two-part ballot showed statehood winning 61% of valid votes, but the format caused confusion. In 2017, only 23% of voters participated. In 2020, statehood received 52.5% support in a yes/no vote. And in 2024, a new plebiscite was held, this time with non-territorial options clearly defined. Statehood won with 58% of votes. But none of these results have prompted binding Congressional action. These votes have largely served symbolic purposes. They have not produced legislative outcomes nor changed the island's political trajectory. Meanwhile, millions have been spent on pro-statehood lobbying efforts and the creation of a "congressional delegation" under Act 167-2020—often referred to as the "criollo embassy." The delegation has been plagued by legal controversies, resignations, internal disputes, and lack of impact in Washington.

3. The PNP and the Illusion of Federal Salvation

The New Progressive Party (PNP) advocates for Puerto Rico's admission as the 51st state. Founded in 1967 as a breakaway faction from the statehood-wing of the Republican Party in Puerto Rico, it has evolved into a bipartisan coalition, though its leadership today includes both Democrats and Republicans. The PNP has governed for many of those years and has failed to propose serious fiscal reforms or structural changes. Instead, it has presided over increased public debt, declining public trust, and bureaucratic inefficiency. From a libertarian perspective, the problem with the PNP is not its goal—it's its method. The party promotes a version of statehood rooted in entitlement rather than readiness. It seeks federal equality without institutional competence. It expects Washington to fix what San Juan refuses to reform. That contradiction weakens its message. True statehood requires demonstrating the capacity to function as a state.

4. The PPD and the Management of Dependency

The Popular Democratic Party (PPD), architect of the Commonwealth status in 1952, has long resisted change. Though it has governed much of Puerto Rico's modern era, the party has failed to update its formula or articulate a realistic alternative. Proposals for an "enhanced ELA" have varied over the years—some calling for greater autonomy, others for permanent union without full integration. None have gained traction in Congress. Like the PNP, the PPD has overseen public deficits, clientelism, and a regulatory maze. Unlike the PNP, it does not even pretend to pursue parity or structural reform. It governs dependency and justifies it through populist rhetoric. While some within the PPD have floated ideas about sovereign association or status modernization, the party has yet to agree on a coherent plan or message. And without clarity, its proposal remains a form of managed ambiguity.

5. The PIP: Independence Without Capacity

The Puerto Rican Independence Party (PIP) has always been a minority force. Founded in 1946 with a democratic socialist platform, it has advocated for decolonization through full sovereignty. Over time, it has aligned with the Socialist International and embraced progressive "woke" causes. Its policy proposals often rely on reparations from the U.S., economic redistribution, and a large state apparatus. The PIP makes noise disproportionate to its electoral strength. Like many ideological movements, it finds support among university youth, intellectual circles, and cultural elites. But its roadmap lacks practical grounding. Independence would require rewriting the constitution, building institutions from scratch, managing borders, handling currency, and renegotiating economic treaties. From a libertarian standpoint, sovereignty begins with institutional discipline and market reform, not slogans. Some support for independence does exist outside the left, particularly among nationalist or right-leaning sectors, but these voices remain fragmented and marginal in the broader debate.

6. The Free Association Mirage

A fourth formula has emerged in recent years: the Free Associated Republic. Promoted under names like "Estado Libre Soberano" or "República Asociada," it proposes a bilateral compact with the U.S., modeled after the relationships with Micronesia, Palau, or the Marshall Islands. Proponents promise sovereignty with citizenship, autonomy with aid. In theory, it offers dignity without detachment. In practice, it suffers from ambiguity and overreach. Congressional appetite for such a deal is low, and the U.S. has not signaled any interest in opening negotiations. Most versions fail to define key issues: citizenship, defense, trade, immigration, and federal programs. From a libertarian view, the proposal seeks to maximize benefits while minimizing responsibility. Without institutional reform, free association is not a solution—it's a repackaged dependency.

7. A Libertarian Critique of the Status Debate

Puerto Rico's status dilemma is not merely a legal or political problem—it is a symptom of deeper institutional stagnation. While political leaders debate sovereignty, statehood, or free association, few address the root issues: a bloated public sector, fragile rule of law, overregulation, and an economic system sustained by external transfers rather than internal productivity. Each political status is presented as a silver bullet. Statehood is offered as an upgrade; independence, as moral vindication; and free association, as a balanced compromise. But none of these formulas guarantee prosperity or liberty without foundational reform. Any non-colonial path will require: - Simplifying and modernizing the tax code—potentially replacing income taxes with consumption-based models like VAT or land value taxation. - Decentralizing government through municipal autonomy, inspired by competitive federalism. - Reducing bureaucracy and professionalizing public service. - Restoring the integrity of law enforcement, the judiciary, and public procurement. - Negotiating the repeal or modification of harmful federal constraints, such as the Jones Act, which limits maritime trade and raises consumer costs. These are not partisan goals—they are preconditions for self-governance. Without them, Puerto Rico will remain economically weak, politically irrelevant, and permanently dependent, regardless of its status.

8. Reform and Responsibility: A Path Forward

Puerto Rico has not lacked votes, commissions, or diagnoses—it has lacked political will. While status dominates headlines, the deeper deficit is one of institutional credibility. No matter what path the island pursues, it must begin by confronting the internal decay of its governance model. Today, over 40% of Puerto Rico's budget comes from federal transfers. Nearly half of its population lives in poverty. The labor participation rate remains one of the lowest under U.S. jurisdiction. This dependency weakens Puerto Rico's position, not just economically, but politically. In Washington, the island is often treated as a peripheral, unserious actor: a Caribbean ward, not a peer. In contrast, other states—richer or poorer—have asserted their interests through fiscal discipline, legal strength, and cultural cohesion. Texas, Florida, Utah, and the Dakotas exemplify models of decentralization and growth. Puerto Rico must move in that direction. Reform is not a partisan wish—it's a requirement. True sovereignty—whether within a federation or outside it—means owning the consequences of self-government. That includes confronting debt, restructuring the energy sector, modernizing education, fixing pensions, and restoring trust in institutions. It also means ending the political theater of permanent dependence and building a society where dignity stems from responsibility, not rhetoric. For Puerto Rico to be respected, it must first learn to respect itself. Not with slogans or symbolic laws, but with competence, discipline, and vision. That is the path forward. And that is what liberty demands.

The views expressed in this chapter reflect the author's independent analysis and do not necessarily represent the position of the editor or other contributors.

References:

Economic and Fiscal Landscape

1. Federal Reserve Bank of New York – Puerto Rico Economic Indicators (May 2025)

Provides detailed data on employment, income, and industry trends, highlighting progress in private sector growth and stabilization of household delinquencies.

2. News is My Business – Puerto Rico Faces Economic, Social Challenges in 2025–2029

Analyzes current challenges such as high energy costs, demographic shifts, and the need for strategic policy decisions to revitalize economic growth.

3. Trading Economics – Puerto Rico GDP Forecast

Projects Puerto Rico's GDP to reach $119.67 billion by the end of 2025, offering insights into economic growth expectations.

Statehood and Political Representation

4. Council on Foreign Relations – Puerto Rico: A US Territory in Crisis

Discusses the implications of statehood, including potential increases in federal benefits and the political dynamics involved.

Explores the economic and political benefits of statehood, emphasizing equal representation and access to federal programs.

Libertarian Perspectives and Policy Recommendations

6. Cato Institute – To Reach Statehood, Puerto Rico Should Improve Its Financial Practices

Advocates for constitutional amendments to ensure balanced budgets and fiscal responsibility as a pathway to statehood.

7. Students For Liberty – Puerto Rico's Failed Experiment

Critiques paternalistic policies and supports free-market solutions to address economic stagnation.

Energy Infrastructure and Modernization

8. AP News – $365M Slated for Solar Projects in Puerto Rico Will Be Diverted to Power Grid

Reports on the reallocation of funds from solar projects to improve the aging power grid, highlighting the complexities of energy policy.

9. Reuters – US Redirects Puerto Rico Solar Power Funds to Oil Plants

Details the shift in energy funding priorities and the implications for Puerto Rico's energy independence and sustainability goals.

References:

Economic and Fiscal Landscape

1. Federal Reserve Bank of New York. *Puerto Rico Economic Indicators: May 2025.* New York: Federal Reserve Bank of New York, 2025. https://www.newyorkfed.org/outreach-and-education/puerto-rico.
2. News is My Business. "Puerto Rico Faces Economic, Social Challenges in 2025–2029." *News Is My Business*, May 2025. https://newsismybusiness.com/puerto-rico-faces-economic-social-challenges-in-2025-2029.
3. Trading Economics. "Puerto Rico GDP Forecast." *TradingEconomics.com*. Accessed May 26, 2025. https://tradingeconomics.com/puerto-rico/gdp.

Statehood and Political Representation

1. Council on Foreign Relations. "Puerto Rico: A U.S. Territory in Crisis." *CFR.org*, 2024. https://www.cfr.org/backgrounder/puerto-rico-us-territory-crisis.

2. PR51st. "Will Statehood Benefit Puerto Rico?" *PR51st.com*. Accessed May 26, 2025. https://www.pr51st.com/will-statehood-benefit-puerto-rico.

Libertarian Perspectives and Policy Recommendations

1. Cato Institute. "To Reach Statehood, Puerto Rico Should Improve Its Financial Practices." *Cato at Liberty (blog)*, 2024. https://www.cato.org/blog/puerto-rico-financial-practices-path-statehood.
2. Students For Liberty. "Puerto Rico's Failed Experiment." *StudentsForLiberty.org*, 2023. https://studentsforliberty.org/blog/puerto-ricos-failed-experiment.

Energy Infrastructure and Modernization

1. Associated Press. "$365M Slated for Solar Projects in Puerto Rico Will Be Diverted to Power Grid." *AP News*, March 2025. https://apnews.com/article/puerto-rico-solar-power-grid-divert.
2. Reuters. "US Redirects Puerto Rico Solar Power Funds to Oil Plants." *Reuters*, March 2025. https://www.reuters.com/business/energy/us-redirects-puerto-rico-solar-funds-oil-2025-03-14.

Note: Grammarly was utilized throughout this book to correct grammar and format references.

---

[1] Smith, Adam. An Inquiry into the Nature and Causes of the Wealth of Nations. London: Methuen & Co., 1776.

[2] Keynes, John Maynard. The General Theory of Employment, Interest and Money. London: Macmillan, 1936.

[3] Hayek, Friedrich A. The Road to Serfdom. Chicago: University of Chicago Press, 1944.

[4] Friedman, Milton. Capitalism and Freedom. Chicago: University of Chicago Press, 1962.

[5] Marx, Karl. Das Kapital. A Critique of Political Economy. Hamburg, Otto Meissner Verlag, 1867.

[6] Federal Reserve Bank of New York. 2025. *Puerto Rico Economic Indicators (May 2025)*. New York: Federal Reserve Bank of New York. https://www.newyorkfed.org/puerto-rico/

[7] Council on Foreign Relations. 2025. *Puerto Rico: A U.S. Territory in Crisis*. Updated January 2025. https://www.cfr.org/backgrounder/puerto-rico-us-territory-crisis

[8] Cato Institute. 2023. *To Reach Statehood, Puerto Rico Should Improve Its Financial Practices*. Washington, D.C.: Cato Institute. https://www.cato.org/blog/reach-statehood-puerto-rico-should-improve-its-financial-practices

[9] Council on Foreign Relations, "Puerto Rico: A U.S. Territory in Crisis," January 8, 2025, https://www.cfr.org/backgrounder/puerto-rico-us-territory-crisis.

[10] Center for Economic and Policy Research, "Puerto Rico's Colonial Legacy and its Continuing Economic Troubles," https://cepr.net/publications/puerto-ricos-colonial-legacy-and-its-continuing-economic-troubles/.

[11] Ojel L. Rodríguez Burgos, "Puerto Rico's Struggle for Liberty," Law & Liberty, https://lawliberty.org/puerto-ricos-struggle-for-liberty/

[12] The Real News Network, "The Unelected Board Perpetuating Colonialism in Puerto Rico," https://therealnews.com/promesa-and-colonialism-in-puerto-rico.

[13] Princeton University Library, "The Story Behind Limited Voting Rights in Puerto Rico," April 2024, https://specialcollections.princeton.edu/2024/04/the-puerto-rican-commonwealth-the-aclu-and-the-u-s-government-the-story-behind-limited-voting-rights-in-puerto-rico/

[14] Hispanic Federation, *Response of the Federal Government to Hurricane Maria in Puerto Rico* (2021), https://www.hispanicfederation.org/wp-content/uploads/2024/07/Response-of-the-Federal-Government-2021.pdf.

[15] Instituto de Libertad Económica, *Will Puerto Rico Be Able to Survive Without Federal Aid?*, https://institutodelibertadeconomica.org/en/publications/will-puerto-rico-be-able-to-survive-without-federal-aid/.

[16] UCF Global Perspectives, *The Jones Act and Puerto Rico* (2024), https://ucfglobalperspectives.org/blog/2024/03/28/the-jones-act-and-puerto-rico/.

[17] Ibid.

[18] Institute for Policy Innovation (IPI), *Formulating a Pro-Growth Economic Strategy for Puerto Rico*, https://www.ipi.org/ipi_issues/detail/leave-no-state-or-territory-behind-formulating-a-pro-growth-economic-strategy-for-puerto-rico.

[19] "Puerto Rico: A U.S. Territory In Crisis," Council On Foreign Relations, last modified June 5, 2025, https://www.cfr.org/backgrounder/puerto-rico-us-territory-crisis.

[20] AP News, "$365M Slated For Solar Projects In Puerto Rico Will Be Diverted To Power Grid," last modified June 5, 2025, https://apnews.com/article/puerto-rico-solar-grid.

[21] Milton Friedman, Capitalism and Freedom (Chicago: University of Chicago Press, 1962).

[22] Tarmo Kalvet, "Innovation Policy Challenges in a Small Country: The Case of Estonia," Technology in Society 29, no. 4 (2007): 405–421.

[23] Sebastian Edwards, Left Behind: Latin America and the False Promise of Populism (Chicago: University of Chicago Press, 2010), 88–91.

[24] Cato Institute, "To Reach Statehood, Puerto Rico Should Improve Its Financial Practices," Cato at Liberty, 2024, https://www.cato.org

[25] News is My Business. "Puerto Rico Faces Economic, Social Challenges in 2025–2029." Accessed June 2, 2025. https://newsismybusiness.com/puerto-rico-economic-social-challenges-2025-2029/.

[26] Council on Foreign Relations. "Puerto Rico: A U. S. Territory in Crisis." Accessed June 2, 2025. https://www.cfr.org/backgrounder/puerto-rico-us-territory-crisis.

[27] **Cato Institute.** *Cato Institute 2021 Annual Report*. Washington, D.C.: Cato Institute, 2021. https://www.cato.org/sites/cato.org/files/2022-12/2021-annual-report-revised.pdf.

[28] Cato Institute, "To Reach Statehood, Puerto Rico Should Improve Its Financial Practices," accessed June 8, 2025, https://www.cato.org/blog/reach-statehood-puerto-rico-should-improve-its-financial-practices.

[29] US Government Accountability Office, Puerto Rico: Factors Contributing to the Debt Crisis and Potential Federal Actions to Address Them, GAO-18-387 (Washington, D.C. 2018), accessed at https://www.gao.gov/products/gao-18-387.

[30] Congressional Research Service, Puerto Rico's Political Status and the 2017 Referendum, R44721 (January 10, 2017), accessed at https://crsreports.congress.gov/product/pdf/R/R44721.

[31] US Congressional Budget Office, Federal Taxes Paid by Residents of Puerto Rico and Other Territories, April 2020, https://www.cbo.gov/publication/56376.

[32] US Government Accountability Office, Puerto Rico: Information on How Statehood Would Potentially Affect Selected Federal Programs and Revenue Sources, GAO-14-31 (Washington, D.C., 2014), https://www.gao.gov/products/gao-14-31.

[33] Robert W. Larson, _New Mexico's Quest for Statehood, 1846-1912_ (Albuquerque: University of New Mexico Press, 1968)

[34] US Government Accountability Office, Puerto Rico: Factors Contributing to the Debt Crisis and Potential Federal Actions to Address Them, GAO-18-387 (Washington, D.C., 2018), https://www.gao.gov/products/gao-18-387.

[35] Christina D. Ponsa-Kraus, "Political Wine in a Judicial Bottle: Justice Sotomayor's Surprising Concurrence in Aurelius," Harvard Law Review 134, no. 2 (2020): 508–541.

[36] US House of Representatives, Puerto Rico Status Act, H.R. 8393, 117th Congress (2022), https://www.congress.gov/bill/117th-congress/house-bill/8393.

[37] The Department of Justice took the unusual step of sharing its Puerto Rico findings in a mid-summer 2019 release. Those notes were indexed under Public Corruption in Puerto Rico and now rest in the agencys archived news room.

[38] National Center for Education Statistics, *Puerto Rico Overview*, 2024, https://nces.ed.gov/nationsreportcard/stateprofile/overview/pr

[39] EdChoice, *Free School Selection Program – Puerto Rico*, accessed 2025, https://www.edchoice.org/school-choice/programs/puerto-rico/

[40] Education Policy meta-analysis, EdChoice outcomes, Journalists' Resource

[41] EdChoice via Journalists' Resource, *Private School Vouchers*, accessed 2025, https://journalistsresource.org/education/private-school-vouchers-school-choice-research-2/

[42] *Puerto Rico Status Act*, S.3231/H.R.2757––118th Cong. (2023–2024), November6,2023, Congress.gov.

[43] Alberto M. Burgos-Rivera,*Elite Settlements in Island Territories: The Road to a Binding Political Status Referendum in New Caledonia and Puerto Rico*, Island Studies Journal 18, no.2 (2023): 186–206. islandstudiesjournal.org

[44] *Puerto Rico's Plebiscites,* Puerto Rico Report, March 13,2025, PuertoRicoReport.com.

[45] 1967 Referendum: *Puerto Rico's plebiscites have demonstrated shifting public sentiment.* In 1967, voters unanimously favored maintaining commonwealth status (60.4%), while 38.8% selected statehood. See "Puerto Rico's Plebiscites," *Puerto Rico Report*, November 13, 2024

[46] *Ibid.* On the 1993 referendum, statehood nearly matched commonwealth support (46.6% vs. 48.9%).

[47] *Ibid.* The 1998 vote showed strong dissatisfaction with existing options; "none of the above" beat statehood (50.5% vs. 46.6%)

[48] Puerto Rico Statehood Referendum (2020)," *Ballotpedia*—noting a 61.2% vote for statehood in 2012.

[49] *Ballotpedia*, "Puerto Rico Statehood Referendum (2020).

[50] *Puerto Rico Report*, "Understanding the 2024 Puerto Rico Plebiscite Results," Jan. 24–26, 2025.

[51] Robert J. Holsworth, "Positive Non-interventionism and the Cowperthwaite Legacy," *Historical Review* 45, no. 2 (2014)

[52] "Hong Kong Economic Freedom," *Fraser Institute*, 2024 Index of Economic Freedom, https://www.fraserinstitute.org.

[53] Andrea Kendall-Taylor and Erica Frantz, *How Dictatorships Work* (Cambridge: Cambridge University Press, 2016)

[54] Jonathan Sullivan and Edmund W. Cheng, "Freedom's Fall in Hong Kong," *Hoover Institution*, 2021.

[55] "From State to Market: Thirty Years of Economic Success in Estonia," Friedrich Naumann Foundation, 2020.

Don't miss out!

Visit the website below and you can sign up to receive emails whenever Jose Rivera Neris publishes a new book. There's no charge and no obligation.

https://books2read.com/r/B-A-UNMTD-DXKQG

BOOKS 2 READ

Connecting independent readers to independent writers.

Also by Jose Rivera Neris

Politics

The 51st State: A Libertarian path for Puerto Rico's Economic Revival and Statehood

Social Studies

The Facts, Ethics, and Culture of Strip Clubs

About the Author

With over 14 years in the US Army and as a Federal employee, Jose Rivera Neris is a political scientist, author, and military veteran. He earned both a Bachelor's and Master's degree in Political Science with an emphasis on conflict studies, governance, and social justice from American Military University. His interdisciplinary master's degree combines professional security practice with critical, human rights, and historiographical theories. Jose is currently pursuing another Master's degree in Global History.

Jose focuses his research on labor and culturally constructed social problems pertaining to, and the communities on, which there is minimal documentation. Jose's works are informed by the desire to help reframe problematic perceptions, particularly those pertaining to the dancers and sex workers. Jose comprehensively examines social problems and equips himself with academic knowledge, which ensures his writing is fact based, straightforward, and empathetic.

Jose is also a member of the District of Columbia National Guard and is currently stationed at Fort Bliss, Texas. He is still working on his provocative, informative, and inspiring essays. Jose aims to inspire judgment suspension through this book, one person at a time.

www.ingramcontent.com/pod-product-compliance
Lightning Source LLC
LaVergne TN
LVHW090420210926
848480LV00002B/632
* 9 7 9 8 2 3 1 0 0 9 5 6 5 *